Decisions
Decide
Destiny

Kevin Mullens

FZM Publishing
PO Box 3707
Hickory, NC 28603

ISBN
978-0-9891997-4-2

Printed in the United States of America

TABLE OF CONTENT

FOREWARD

When I sit down and ponder all of the people I've met and had the privilege of getting to know, one man in particular makes my heart swell with joy and honor. That man is Kevin Mullens.

My first impression of Kevin was he is a "GO GETTER." He is passionate about success and how to help others be successful. After getting to know him better and becoming friends, I realize that Kevin is more than a successful millionaire. He is more than a father, a husband and a friend to others. He is a gift from God to us. God has anointed Kevin with the passion and burden to help others find Biblical Prosperity.

There's no better way to live life except in the blessings and favor of God. Kevin has become a voice to the nations on how we can fulfill our God divine gifts and purpose. So many people walk through life void and empty, simply because they got caught up in a system of earning a living; not understanding that they were created to live life, not earn one.

In Kevin's newest manuscript, "Decision Decide Wealth," you're going to unlock the keys necessary to conquer the mundane, just existing life and walk into the divine power of increase. It is my recommendation that all those who embark on the journey of reading this powerful manuscript take in every word. Read it slowly... read it daily... take it to your devotional time... write down its keys and watch your life explode into an even greater meaning than just existing. **You decide your future. No one can decide it for you!**

Dr. Jerry A Grillo, Jr.
Author and Speaker

Introduction

The idea of victory, success or triumph is something everyone has thought of at some time in their life. Everyone has had a dream of doing something that would not only impact their lives, but the lives of those that surround them. Most people spend their entire lives talking about what they are going to do, but rarely get around to doing anything. Constantly using words like ONE DAY, SOME DAY, ALMOST, or TOMMOROW to describe their time frame for committing to doing something different so they can get something different. Statistics prove that people generally never regret the things they did do. Instead, they tend to regret the things they didn't do. Out of seven days in a week we know that SOMEDAY just isn't one of them. The Word of God says that TODAY is the day of salvation. You have the ability to make a decision right now to move away from that dark hole that holds you captive from having a breakthrough!

You can do something about it today.

I often hear the infamous words "I WILL TRY," after training or teaching tools for success. It is time we put the words "I' WILL TRY" to rest. Believers in Christ should get rid of the *"I will try to change"* or *"I will try to succeed"* attitude. We are giving ourselves permission to fail when we use these words. As Yoda so famously stated, **"Do or do not.** There is NO try."

The word 'try' is almost as disempowering as the word 'can't.' It shows a lack of belief in a positive outcome and a lack of belief in one's self to get the job done no matter how many times it takes. We often quote scripture like, *"Greater is He that is in me than he that is in the world,"* or, *"I can do ALL things through Christ which strengthens me,"* yet we shrink under the pressure that comes with success or victory when confronted with opportunity to make a difference.

Instead of having the attitude that we will *TRY* we should start using empowering phrases like, *I CAN, I WILL, I AM* or *I DID.* Can you see the difference words make as we embark on the journey of being an overcomer, a doer, and a difference maker?

One of my mentors, Paul Orberson, would say, *"You try peas and carrots, but you do this."* Art Williams would say, *"Just do it."* Our challenge is realizing the greatest enemy we will ever face is ourselves. The battle rages inwardly everyday between remaining positive and upbeat or being depressed and discouraged by our circumstances. It will require great discipline to truly succeed at anything, but with unwavering faith in what God has already promised us as children of the Most High, we all have the ability to accomplish whatever we set out to do. Our inadequacies are inferior to the potential for greatness that lies within each of us. We were made in His image therefore the very DNA of a sovereign God resides in each of us just waiting to be released.

As we take this journey together, you will find the courage to stand tall in the middle of chaos, crisis, or adversity, and recognize the authority you truly have to be the architect of your own destiny—the CEO of your own life. You alone have the power to create a world where you can walk in favor, increase, and over flow based on the decisions you make TODAY. No longer will we tolerate procrastination based on fears that hold us back.

CHAPTER ONE

INDECISION
IS THE DOOR TO FAILURE!

Success is rewarding... Success is a gift... Success is everything that is awesome and good, but success is never easy! Success is the result of those who can learn how to pick themselves up off the floor of defeat and pain, and get back to living a God centered life.

We must get this in our understanding that success was not supposed to be a flowerbed of ease. If it were easy, then everyone would be successful or victorious. You will fail many times along the way but remember King David's words...

"As I walk THROUGH the valley of the shadow of death I will fear no evil." Psalm 23:4

We are responsible for getting up when we fall and continue to move forward. God is able to keep the promises He has made. Our responsibility is to believe and stagger not through unbelief. You are closer than you think, so take courage, and from this day forward call those things that are not, as though they already are. It's your turn to experience all of the blessings that God has in store for you and to become the person you were meant to be—the person you were predestined to be.

11

5 Reasons You Procrastinate:

1. INDECISION

"There is no more miserable human being than one in whom nothing is habitual but indecision." William James

The Bible says in James 1:8 " that, *"a double minded man is unstable in all his ways."* Indecision keeps us from many blessings because we are always putting off tomorrow what can be done today. Napoleon Hill wrote in the wonderful book, "Think and Grow Rich," that there is a quality all billionaires have in common, and that is the ability to make a quick and decisive decision and also stick to it. Yes, making irrational decisions can often come with consequences, but when we are well informed and have the maturity to see a good opportunity, there is no reason to set idly by and do NOTHING when we have the ability to capitalize NOW. By nature we live with indecision. Have you ever decided to go out with your friends, and once you get in the car you spend the next thirty minutes driving around town saying, *"Where do you want to eat?"*

"I don't know, where do you want to eat?"

Then when we finally make up our minds on where to eat, we do the exact same thing upon ordering food, *"What are you going to eat?"*

Indecision is like coming to the crossroads and being filled with such uncertainty you cannot make up your mind. It's like we are afraid to just make a decision, so we spend most of our time waiting on others to make one for us. This generally leads to us living the life determined by others rather than taking ownership of our own lives by being a decision maker.

Most people often choose to do nothing when confronted with choices. Playing small or always playing safe is the decision of the masses, which will always give you what they have. The choices of kings, leaders, or CEO`s is what separates them from the pack. They do what others are unwilling to do or too afraid to do; therefore they have what others will never have. Decisions decide wealth, so start making decisions today that can radically impact your life in a profound way. Will you decide to stay inside and lay in bed instead of getting up and exercising 20-30 minutes no matter how inconvenient it may seem? Will you ever read or listen to audio books or start reading God's Word so you will be equipped for the battles that lie ahead? Will you always buy tickets to go watch other grown men play a sport they love, always being a spectator, or will you decide to get involved in the game of life and go compete for your family? Do we stay home when we are more than able to go to work or church?

We are faced every single day with small decisions that impact our lives in a huge way so from this day forward stop taking the easy way out. Decide today that will you be a victim of your circumstances or a product of past decisions NO MORE.

Many times I will hear Christians say, *"Lord if you do such and such then I will know I am supposed to do this."* Always trivializing every decision by wanting the angels to come down from glory and declare that they are on the right track.

In the scripture, there were times that certain believers would put a fleece before the Lord. A fleece was basically them asking God for a SIGN that would direct their path. This type of prayer is an easy out as we place everything on hold waiting on something supernatural to happen in order

13

to make a decision. I am not discounting the need for direction or that we shouldn't pray about things, but one must realize that God has blessed us with the ability to make decisions. The spirit of God is living within us as our guide. Having to see a sign is not always a good thing. In Matthew 16:4, Jesus answered them and said, *"A wicked and adulterous generation seeketh after a sign."* So we can see that there comes a time we must trust God to lead us and bless the work we do. We already make decisions everyday with no thought given like which gas station to stop at or what color tie to wear. No sign is needed for these simple decisions. It is only when we are faced with a decision that makes us uncomfortable or requires change. It is in these moments we sometimes create a tactic to stall.

When you think about it, making no decision or indecision is still a decision. The footsteps of the righteous are ordered of the Lord. You will fail, you will learn, and as you learn you will then teach. Take control of your destiny by deciding today to make the hard choices needed to get back on the straight and narrow that few are traveling. I know its tough; it's supposed to be tough.

"Most people will lose more to indecision than they will to a bad decision." Andrew Carnegie.

This is not only the truth; it is the number one reason people remain unsuccessful in their lives. Even unsuccessful people are aware of this principle and its results, but remain unconvinced of how powerful decisions are and how debilitating indecision can be.

I build teams, and I have witnessed people losing millions of potential revenue, because they were unable to make decision on more than one occasion. You have prayed all your life for certain things to happen, so stop being surprised when God answers you. Be more attentive to the things happening everyday on your behalf. Walk away from the darkness of indecision. It is one on the greatest enemies of success and the reason for failure. Today is the day that you will look back and remember you stopped being conflicted about what to do and just decided to make the necessary changes and decisions to be a champion.

2. PERFECTIONISM

If you are the person that is waiting on perfect conditions to get something done then you are going to be waiting forever. I am around people every day who say they want the same things, but few ever accomplish what they set out for. As I mentor, train, and work alongside large groups, all headed seemingly in the right direction, I've noticed that the ones that truly succeed are the ones that get out there from day one and embrace the entire journey as a learning process. The ones who wait until they think they know every answer or attend every training seminar before they get active are the ones that typically get around to doing nothing.

Perfectionism is a society of people that often live in a state of self-doubt and frustration based on certain results and although it sounds noble to want things perfect, it can be a crutch for often doing nothing. A perfectionist tends to focus on failure, or the fear of failure. They never put themselves out there to fall on their face or come up short in regards to their own expectations which can lead to depressing thoughts such as, *"I'm not good enough."*

Those that really succeed have put themselves out there for others to see their vulnerability and even shortcomings. Your authentic story of falling and getting back up inspires others to believe that there is hope for them too. If you consider yourself to be a perfectionist, I urge you to start seizing the moment without fear that you cannot control every aspect of the journey. If you are not careful you will sit paralyzed, always wondering what others think or over analyzing things to the point that you miss a chance to watch the spectacular happen. How many times do we talk about wishing we could go back and invest in Google stock or Apple stock years ago when it was first being offered? I grew up hearing the story of my grandfather having the chance to buy beachfront property in Panama City Beach, Florida back in the early forties. Of course, he didn't make the decision to do so, either because he couldn't see the value or just plain indecision. However, just because my grandfather chose not to purchase does not change the fact the SOMEBODY DID.

How many times in life have you wished you had a do-over? A chance to DO SOMETHING rather than sitting by as a spectator watching others change their life. It is easy to keep making excuses over and over again, but there comes a time we must step up and take charge of our destiny by having the courage to do what often makes us uncomfortable. The road well-traveled is easy for a reason. Even the scripture says the broad way leads to destruction. Can you imagine a book called, *"The 10 Hardest Ways to Lose Weight,"* or, *"The 10 Most Difficult Ways to Change Your Life?"* In America we tend to like it if it's easy, but if it's not then we don't.

"Farmers who wait for perfect weather NEVER plant. If they watch every cloud, they NEVER harvest." Ecclesiastes 11:4 (NLT)

The truth is that perfect conditions rarely exist. You just need to get out there and start swimming upstream against the tide of normalcy and dare to be different. Dare to think outside of the box and be a part of something bigger than you. Creating a movement or revolution always starts with one. That ONE person needs to be you. Stop being the person that complains about government or local issues but never votes or rallies behind anything to make a difference. Stop waiting on change and go be the change.

"Don't wait on leaders, DO IT ALONE, person to person." Mother Teresa

It's easy to say things like, *when I get more money, when I have more time, when the kids are out of school, when I finish my degree*, but there comes a time when we must decide. Decisions decide wealth. What decisions will you start making today that will have a positive impact on your life? These decisions will also affect the lives of those waiting on you to show them it's ok to dream, to be different, to fail and fail again pursuing the things that will change the dynamics of your family's finances forever. We often stand still because we think we are unprepared or don't have the proper skill set yet. You need to realize that *"repetition is king"* which means you will become better at anything through consistency of effort. Read books, attend revivals or business seminars, and connect with successful people that are of like mind and like faith so you gather the skills necessary to accelerate your growth. I love the Zig Ziglar's quote, *"You don't have to be great to get started but you have to get started in order to be great."*

Right now you have something that you are just too afraid to do so you remain paralyzed, but you need to realize that you are more than able. As Joshua and Caleb said, *"We are well able."* The Bible said they had a different spirit. You are a child of God with the very spirit of Christ living within you. *All things are possible to him that believes (Mark 9:23)* so there is no reason for you to wait any longer on perfect conditions. The enemy says wait, later on, next year, but the scripture tells us that TODAY is the day of salvation, so make a decision TODAY to start living an abundant life. Choose to meet adversity and fear of change head on with a newfound faith and resolve that no longer will you serve the master called procrastination, but today you choose what you want and with a burning desire have an unusual determination to see it through.

3. FEAR

"For God has not given us the spirit of fear; but of power, and of love and of a sound mind." 2 Timothy 1:7

This is a scripture often quoted among believers. Saying something doesn't necessarily mean we believe it. We are overcomers because Christ already overcame. Accepting Him as Lord allows Him to take His place in the throne room of our hearts. This gives us the faith to encounter any enemy and know there is no need to fear because when the enemy comes in like a flood, the spirit of the Lord shall lift up a standard against him on our behalf. I want you to ask yourself, *"What am I afraid of?"* What is it that keeps you where you are in life without progress? Fear hinders our ability to make any decision and typically when we do make a decision we make the wrong one because that's generally the easiest.

Proverbs 29:25 (NLT) says, *"Fearing people is a dangerous trap."* What are you currently postponing? The word post-pone means to put off to a later time or delay. How long will you stay in the valley of indecision waiting on things to just get better? You say you have a vision, but vision without execution is hallucination. No vision is poverty in disguise. Many of you have had great ideas, maybe even inventions created within your mind that would work and possibly generate life changing income or help change the world, but fear says, I can't, I don't trust patents, I won't be able to get funding, or it will eventually come out anyway. Sure enough, later on we see what was vivid in our minds on the shelf at our local stores.

The creative power of God, who is unlimited, resides in us waiting on us to reflect His nature, but fear causes us to suppress and silence that inner voice calling us to walk boldly into our destiny. Instead, we settle for the path of least resistance, missing chances left and right to be a difference maker. We are subject to our own thoughts. This is why I am constantly reminding people to guard their thoughts because thoughts become words, and words create the reality we live in.

Job said, *"The thing I greatly feared has come upon me"* Job 3:25. *(KJV)* Job brought forth and manifested that which he feared. We never attract what we want. We would all have a different home, car and bank account if we attracted what we want. We attract what we are! Whatever your dominant thoughts are is what manifests itself in your life. The thing Job feared the most is what happened so we must learn to discipline our thoughts to only think on positive things.

Bob Proctor says, *"Your current bank account is the physical manifestation of you previous thoughts."* This lends proof to the idea that our thoughts determine what we have or don't have. Remove all worry and stress within your mind, pull out all the weeds that suffocate the growth of a positive mindset, because without the right mental attitude towards God's promises, none of them will come to pass. If you will conquer fear through DAILY ACTION towards a specific goal you will see how quickly the world will step aside to let you pass. You don't have to be a mathematician to understand there would be a problem if five percent of the worlds' wealth was divided among ninety-five percent of the world's population. If five percent of the world divides among themselves ninety-five percent of the worlds' wealth then the question becomes, *"How do I become a part of the five percent group?"*

What separates these people from the ninety-five percent? The difference between making a little money or a lot is actually a razors edge, but it's that small difference that creates a law of attraction which opens up the floodgates and begins releasing uncommon FAVOR. Favor will produce what labor never can. We must tear down the walls of fear that keep us a prisoner to our circumstances. No one should ever compromise with their circumstances or life if they are producing what they truly want. Change your words and you will change your destiny. You will bring to you what is already in you when you start declaring things as you want them to be and do so with unshakeable faith.

Prophet William Branham preached a message in 1955 called, "LAW," and said, *"Let your testimony always and your thoughts, everything..."* Never permit a negative thought to come in your mind if you can help it. When it starts don't entertain it. Some would say, *"I can't help the thoughts from coming."* That is like the farmer that said he couldn't stop the birds from flying over his place, but he could sure stop them from roosting. You can't help when the thoughts come but don't entertain them.

"Guard your heart above all else, for it DETERMINES THE COURSE OF YOUR LIFE." Proverbs 4:23 (NLT)

Solomon also conveyed to us that as a man thinks in his heart, so is he. It is becoming clearer how careful we must be with what we allow to enter our mind and heart. If you consider the power of what you just read it sheds light on why we cannot afford to even entertain one negative or contrary thought. Whatever we allow to enter our hearts determines our course of life. This is the difference maker between existing and living a pressed down, shaken together and running over, blessed, and highly favored life. You are going to manifest your most dominant thoughts so be more determined than ever before to think only on what you desire and what has been promised to you in God's Word. You must remember that the creative power within you is going to fully manifest whatever image you give the most attention to. This is why I often say to my business partners and team, *"You are as you say you are."*

You are whatever you repeatedly do or declare. The poverty mindset lives by the idea that *"Life just happens"* or *"Whatever happens will happen,"* but the successful believe, I CREATE MY LIFE.

No more postponing or delaying because of fear. Confess your desires. Jesus is the High Priest of our confession. He can only do for us as we accept His word, believe it and then CONFESS it. Go write down all the things you have wanted to accomplish. Maybe you have a bucket list of things you would like to do but are currently out of your reach. Write down why you haven't done them, and what has held you back. Money, time, etc. Start creating a plan of ACTION that will allow you the freedom to pursue the things you are passionate about.

Many of us have others watching our every move, so cast fear aside and dare to live out your dreams. The dream stealers and negative "Debbie Downers" will always be courtside rooting for you to fail, but put one foot in front of the other and claim what is rightfully yours. Watch others begin to realize that if you can do it so can they. *"Annuit Coeptis"* is a saying on the back of the American dollar. It means *"Providence or God Favors Bold Enterprise."*

God foreordained and chose you to live a fulfilled life with no limitations. The business world favors the bold, the brave, and the fearless. Christ has risen and lives in the heart of man. Greater is He that is in you than in anything you fear, so I want you to attack life. Be a bold witness for the Kingdom and the things that you are passionate about. Watch God unfold Himself in a manner for you to experience His uncommon favor. All that God has promised is rightfully yours, but unbelief will disqualify you. Step out of the boat and obey the voice of Jesus saying, "COME." The wind and sea may rage, but they have no hold on you once you realize that you are holding the hand of Him that holds eternity. There is a Deity living within you waiting to express His being through you. All fear and doubt will leave and only faith will remain when you identify your oneness with Him. Faith activates the promises of God.

4. DISTRACTION

The battle for your success is always going to be over your focus. Situations... crisis... losses... pain... just about everything has a voice and is trying to get your attention. The problem with other voices is that they may be attempting to distract you from your present focus. I have always said that the enemy to your future is the thing or person who tries to break your focus. Broken focus is the reason many fail in life.

It's definitely hard to stay focused when it's so easy to access distraction. TV, Internet, News, Social Networks, and Gossip corners all seem to willingly feed our unproductive side of garbage that keeps us distracted.

"Deferred Gratitude" is a phrase often used in the world of doctors and lawyers to describe how they stayed focused in order to get a degree that can take a long time to achieve. It simply means one's ability to give up partying, new expensive clothes, new car debt, and maybe even skip spring break or summer break, in order to remain focused on finishing their degree. While most people find a way to always stay right where they are, successful people are willing to make the sacrifices others are unwilling to make.

Upon receiving their degree in these specific high paying fields, these people can indulge with a new car, home, toys, etc. because they have now positioned themselves to earn the kind of money that can afford the things they want.

The Olympic athlete has been disciplined and undistracted since his/her youth with aspirations of winning a Gold medal. Literally, the difference in training and focus can mean the difference in millions earned versus millions lost. Bruce Lee said that a warrior is an average man with Laser-Like FOCUS. Psalms 119:1 (the message) says, *"You're blessed when you stay on course...,"* giving us understanding that the road map leading to where we have never been requires focus. I meet so many people along the way that desire MORE, but when face to face with the changes that are necessary to acquire the things they want, most find reasons to quit or lay blame for always falling short. Then it becomes easy to say others got lucky. It is true that the harder you work, especially at the right things, the luckier you get.

People may call you obsessed if you relentlessly pursue something where the outcome is favorable because of the drive and ambition you had to accomplish a goal. Obsessed is a word that lazy people call the dedicated. The great Art Williams said, *"Most can stay committed a day or two, some will even stay committed a month or two, but very few will stay committed until the job is finished."* To be obsessed means the domination of ones thoughts or feelings by a persistent idea, image or desire.

How willing are you to become obsessed with getting in shape, financially free, closer to the Lord or whatever it is that you know you need to commit to? Whatever you are completely focused on will determine whether it actually happens or not.

FOCUS can also mean Following One Course Until Successful. This discipline in any particular area through practice and daily activity can give you an edge in the market place. Become the very best you can be at whatever you're dedicated to and surround yourself with those who are great in the areas that you are weak. You can create your very own mastermind group where each person flourishes in a specialized area, and collectively you become an unstoppable force with no rival. This is true in sports, music, higher education, and most definitely in business.

I meet people that will play video games for hours or even days so intensely focused because they have to finish or win. I have witnessed this same focus in one's desire to finish a book or be so captivated by watching a movie that the house could be on fire and they would never know.

We tend to get the results we desire when we really commit to something. The biggest problem is that we are often focused on things that make no impact on living a more productive life; a highly favored and blessed life. Not that

Donald Trump or Warren Buffet don't watch television or surf the internet, but they are rarely engaged in anything that doesn't add value. Most gifted athletes that we love to admire are just athletes that practiced when others went home early or studied film when it wasn't required so they could be well prepared for their mission. Even the Apostle Paul in reference to serving the Lord said, *"I die daily,"* (1 Corinthians 15:31) (KJV), suggesting that yesterday's victory won't suffice for today. Our victory lies in holding steady when everything seems blurred, never doubting your mission although it seems impossible, holding on to an unmovable force, the foundation of your dreams. I love MJ Durkins' statement that, "Wherever your focus goes, the power flows." Many of you today have recently decided to do something about your current situation. May be you made a decision to create generational blessings in your home or leave a legacy. That decision is often started with enthusiasm and great hope. Then we meet adversity or resistance. Too often we begin to crumble and spend more time looking in the rearview mirror then staying focused on what is before us.

Adversity always births supernatural promotion

The size of your enemy is a clue to the size of your next season. The greater the enemy, the greater the reward. If you are facing warfare, it's a good sign that the enemy has discerned your future and doesn't want you reaching your full potential. He knows what you're capable of when you are completely sold out. Nehemiah was a great man, who was full of God. He saw a great need for the temple of God to be rebuilt, and when Nehemiah began to take on that giant feat, his enemy confronted him almost immediately after deciding to lead the great campaign for restoring the temple. The tool of this enemy was distraction. The enemy wanted Nehemiah to come down off the wall he was building for a meeting, but Nehemiah knew their plot so his response was, *"I am doing a GREAT WORK and cannot come down"* Nehemiah 6:3 (The Message).

We could all learn a lesson from Nehemiah. How many times does the enemy show up when we announce our plans to do something great? The enemy doesn't care if you merely exist and live in survival mode. You have no voice when you allow complacency to take over. Maybe you have no income to support your efforts. Lack of motivation doesn't strike fear in the heart of Satan. God is trying to stretch you every day so you will dream bigger, do more, and be more, but we keep finding reason to fail or do nothing. It is time to tell your enemy that you are doing a great work and cannot come down. Do not let the enemy frustrate your purpose. Your destiny calling requires sacrifice, discipline, and focus. You can start today and within three years or less be financially free or maybe even be a ***multi-millionaire***.

You can start today and be in the best shape of your life within two or three years. You can have the Bible read within a year. It's actually amazing how soon we can turn things around when we make up our mind to change. You were designed to dominate and designed to prosper! When you fully commit and find others that will hold you accountable you will soon see that anything is possible. As you stretch yourself and as your vision expands you will see that you were always an eagle ordained to soar the heavens. You just needed to leave the nest of "so called" security to show others the endless possibilities. Your story of triumph is necessary in helping reveal to others that they can leave the barnyard and soar with the eagles too. You will see a new world materialized before you, that actually already existed, with the right mentoring, right mindset, and daily sacrifices. It was waiting on you to come take what is rightfully yours because we do not attract what we want but we attract what we are. Everything in our life we have attracted through dominant thought. You are the manifestation of whatever you confess and truly believe. Like attracts like. Be the person that God has called you to be starting TODAY. Now you can say with authority, *"Satan, get thee behind me."* You can rebuke poverty, sickness, broken homes, and wayward children and with unwavering faith and expectation watch miracles begin to happen. Watch the person you become attract the blessings of God, and attract the type of people you need in your life to enter your next season of increase and overflow.

5. LAZINESS

"Lazy people want much but get little, but those who work hard will prosper." Proverbs 13:4(NLT)

Solomon was a man of great wisdom and wealth; so much so that it surpassed all of the kings in his time. Laziness keeps even those with the right knowledge to prosper bound in their current circumstances when they choose not apply wisdom. There was a word used a lot when I was a kid to describe lazy people and it was, SLACKER. The word slacker by definition means, moving slowly, lacking in activity, not busy. Immediately we all have an image of someone we know that fits this category. They seem to boast of all they are going to do or want to do, but when given the smallest task they seem to display their ingratitude and unthankful nature. I am often touring the country empowering and teaching believers how to create wealth using Kingdom principles, and I am constantly running into the masses that say, "I'm tired of doing the same thing and never getting a different result," or "I'm tired of working two or three jobs and never getting ahead." "Please teach us how to create financial freedom."

It sounds noble but when I give instruction on the certain things that are necessary I begin to hear things like, *"Not that"* or *"Is there another way?"* or *"Can I do something different?"*

Success only comes before work in the dictionary. Procrastination and laziness go hand in hand. One of the requirements to success is to get out of our comfort zone, learn a new skill, read new material, or actually apply the principles we have read in the Bible our entire lives. Solomon said that when a man will not follow instruction, poverty and shame is his (Proverbs 13:18). A protégé must see his future in the life of his mentor. He must be teachable and coachable understanding that his mentor's wisdom can get him to a place he has never been before if he will follow the road map laid out before him. As the great Jim Rohn said, *"Don't be lazy in learning."*

"He becometh poor that dealeth with a slack hand: but the hand of the diligent maketh rich". Proverbs 10:4 KJV

"One who is slack in his work is brother to one who destroys." Proverbs 18:9 NIV

Your Future is Decided by the Learning Curve you can endure:

Have you ever noticed that the same people show up in a church body for events such as praying, fasting, missions, soul winning, community work, or a church clean-up day?

It always seems to be the same people with all the excuses on why they can't participate. These people have not yet learned the laws of **FAVOR**. They also have not figured out the art of giving. People who are possessed by a spirit of laziness get around to doing nothing and rarely make an

28

impact on anything or anyone. They rarely take advantage of opportunities that could change their circumstances in a hurry because it might be hard, require change and most definitely require sacrifice. Successful people do what unsuccessful people are unwilling to and this applies in any field.

Arnold Schwarzenegger said, *"The last three or four reps are what makes the muscle grow."*

This pain divides the champion from someone else who is not a champion. That's what most people lack; having the guts to go on and just say they'll go through the pain no matter what happens.

Now some might argue that Arnold was physically gifted which would be true. However, great athletes separate themselves from other highly talented athletes by the amount of practice and extra labor they put into getting the most out of their God given talent. Everybody might stand, but you can be a standout. Every one of us has the very DNA of God within us. We are all made in His own image. We all have access to the same Bible, same study material and with the help of the internet we have access to every tool imaginable to be the very best we can be. Why do some read God's Word as it relates to prosperity, abundance, increase, etc. and choose to see these promises manifested in their lives by working hard at the right things and others fall into the category of being a hearer of the Word but not a doer of the Word? You can choose right now to accept all that God has in store for you as a rightful joint-heir with Him or you can continue to be a "slacker" doing nothing. The five percent that have created a life of wealth didn't just get lucky. The harder you work the luckier you get. They were committed not only to learning but also applying. Most people have no written goals and the few that do are very lazy on doing the things necessary to reach these goals. I can only imagine the frustration of the great warrior Joshua as he stood before the Israelites knowing they were fully aware of what was promised of them. What should have been only a three day journey from Egypt to Canaan took the children of Israel forty years. Joshua said, *"How long will you be SLACK to go in and possess the land which the Lord, the God of your fathers, has given you?"* (Joshua 18:3). I feel this way today when I am among spirit filled believers that know the scripture; they know the promises of God but continue to just settle for whatever they have. The Promised Land was full of giants that were standing in the way of wealth and freedom and just because it was promised to them did not mean they wouldn't have to fight for every inch of it. Victory is inevitable for the ones who are determined and driven; those who are willing to charge the mountain and refuse to quit. Today, I ask you to believe with a strong faith in all that God has promised you and all that you desire to do. Nothing is impossible with God. He's waiting on you.

The enemy of slack and laziness has allowed the adversary to build circles around us and accomplish much while we sit still wondering what just happened. The world is full of people that are ambitious in causes that believers disagree with. Their level of commitment is unmatched and their passion for wrong fuels the completion of their movement. How long will our unwillingness to get involved allow the enemy to enlarge their territory and enforce their laws and ideology upon us? Decide today to never lose another inch without a fight. I say to you that WE ARE ABLE, and we serve a LIVING GOD. The Word says *"I'll draw nigh to you if you will draw nigh to me (James 4:8),"* so you can see that there is something required of you. You don't need to be the most talented. Hard work beats talent when talent won't work hard. What good would the promise had been to Abraham that wherever the soles of his feet trod would represent ownership if Abraham stayed in his living room? We have sat idle for way to long; a destiny with great purpose awaits you. I am often asked what the secret to my success has been. Everyone has an opinion, but the real story of my success is that once I found something to pour myself into that would yield the highest return and make the greatest impact I OUT WORKED everyone. While still tending to the responsibilities of my traditional business, my ministry, and my family, I just OUT WORKED everyone else. The results were staggering, and the more I pushed myself I realized that the only limitations that existed were the ones I placed on myself. Never make excuses, never accept excuses and always find a way to get it done. I soon found an army of volunteered soldiers that wanted the exact same things I wanted and collectively we become an unstoppable force. Tired? Exhausted? YES. Paul Orberson would say, *"If you're not tired then your dream isn't big enough"*

When you mentally commit to living in your own personal Promised Land, you will not run from the giants, but you will become a giant killer. Fear, distraction, indecision, and laziness will no longer stand between you and your destiny. So put on your work boots and go finish on empty; giving it everything you've got. No matter what, you must FINISH! You are well equipped and anointed for this battle.

"Let us not be weary in well doing; for in due season we shall reap, if we faint not." Galatians 6:9 (KJV)

CHAPTER 2

Recognizing your Position of AUTHORITY

When you accepted Jesus as Lord of your life you accepted all that He is. You became a partaker of all of His wonderful blessings. We are protected by a King who is holding you in the palm of His hand, and He has never lost one of His yet. When we recognize who we really are in the Kingdom of God, we will skip worry and fear and move into complete peace because we are resting on His Word rather than how we feel.

Your enemy has no clue who he is messing with when he attacks you. Genesis 12:3 (KJV) says, *"And I will bless them that bless thee, and curse him that curseth thee:"* How often do we find ourselves in warfare and begin to lose faith when we know the mighty hand of Jehovah is fighting on our behalf. Isaiah 49:25 (KJV) declares, *"For I will contend with him that contendeth with thee;"* once again establishing the strong arm of a God that cannot fail; rousing Himself on your behalf to bring forth victory.

David understood what it was like to be deceived by the enemy who called themselves his friends, right down to his own family. David also knew that the Lord prepared a table for him in the presence of his enemies; showing us that sometimes God calms the storm and other times He calms His child.

David wrote in **Psalms 34:17 (KJV),** *"The righteous cry, and the LORD heareth, and delivereth them out of all their troubles."* Giving us hope that when we lift up our voices He will deliver us from ALL our troubles. David being a man that understood failure and heartache wrote in another place found in Psalm 18:47-48 (KJV), *"It is God that avengeth me, and subdueth the people under me. He delivereth me from mine enemies: yea, thou liftest me up above those that rise up against me:"*

I pray you begin to believe, as one writer wrote, that if God be for us, then who can be against us. We are powerful beyond measure. Not only are you already victorious, but you are an overcomer because Christ already overcame. David hung onto promises like, "He shall give His angels charge over you, to keep you in all your ways," and, "The angel of the Lord encamps all around those who fear Him and delivers them." (Psalms 91:11 & 34:7)

David knew in *Whom* he was trusting. You have no need to fight this battle because God is fighting it for you. Relax yourself and recognize that NO weapon formed against thee shall prosper. From the very beginning God has given us great authority. When we activate God's word with faith we are mighty conquerors.

"Whatsoever ye shall bind on earth shall be bound in heaven: and whatsoever ye shall loose on earth shall be loosed in heaven." Matthew 18:18 (KJV)

The authority of the church or believer should not be in question. When we surrender our lives to Christ we accept His spirit. The Writer of the word is living within us; waiting on us to speak God's Word with boldness and great expectation. The authority we live by is not based on arrogance or emotionalism, but it's based on the knowledge of having a risen Savior living within us *Who* can manifest His word spoken through our lips.

Why do we tolerate so many things in our homes, churches, and personal lives when we know what the Word says? When will we wake up from our slumber and take Canaan? Why sit idle waiting on someone else when we have the ability within ourselves. You are the very reflection of an infallible God that is capable of doing things seemingly impossible. Do not give one inch to the enemy! Never give in to any thought that you are less or incapable!

When an adoption took place scripturally it represented the placing of a son positionally. Meaning you acted in the same authority as your father. **Mark 11:24 (KJV)** says, ***"Therefore I say unto you, what things soever you desire, when you pray, BELIEVE that ye receive them and ye shall have them."***

James teaches us to ask in FAITH, nothing wavering. There are so many areas that we lack in that we don't have to.

SUBDUE

God gave you the AUTHORITY to "subdue" earth. (Genesis 1:28). The word subdues means to *conquer, defeat, overcome. Can't you see you were created to Conquer!*

God designed us to dominate and rule from the beginning besides ordaining us to live an abundant life. We must learn to subdue mountains, systems, fears, and thoughts. The only limitations we face are the ones we place on ourselves by disbelieving what God's word says about us. Be bold in your faith to DECLARE and DECREE all of God's word with authority and watch miracles take place. Jim Rohn says, *"It's easy to be wealthy, it's easy to be successful if we follow a few principles and guard our thoughts daily so our mindset is the same as our God."*

There are no limitations and nothing is impossible. Whatever you desire you can have in prayer if you BELIEVE. So, do you believe? Do you really BELIEVE?

God is a kind and merciful God, but do not think He doesn't expect increase from us. He wonderfully made us in His image to be like Him and to express His nature. Today, you should place under subjection the greatest enemy you will ever face. That enemy of course is YOU. We tend to get in our own way every single time we make a decision to start doing things different in order to get things different. We know what we should do, but applying this knowledge daily requires great sacrifice and discipline which very few are willing to do.

Let's SUBDUE, conquer, and overcome everything opposite of where we are going. Anything that would hinder our destiny must be removed not just suppressed. Christ is the High Priest of our confession so be careful what you confess. Your words literally create the reality you live in. Confess victory, abundance, healing, restoration, and increase. Whatever you say determines who you are so be careful what you utter.

Daniel, the prophet, wrote about a group of warriors who knew who they were and *Whom* they served. Daniel 11:32 says, *"But the people WHO KNOW THEIR GOD shall be strong, and carry out exploits."* Notice he said, "Those who KNOW their God."

To be born again simply means to have Jesus Christ personally revealed to you and to have a personal relationship with Him. You must be fully confident that you have accepted Christ and all of His Word. To know Him is to also know His will for your life. Moses said in Exodus 33:13, *"God show me your ways that I may know You."* He didn't say, *"I just want to get into the Promised Land and be remembered as the greatest leader of all time."* Moses said, *"The most important thing is that I know Your ways; that I know You."*

This is similar to the prayer that the apostle Paul prayed for the church in Ephesians 1:17. *"That the God of our Lord Jesus Christ, the Father of glory, may give unto you the spirit of wisdom and revelation in the knowledge of him."*

It is my prayer that you start experiencing Jesus in the most intimate way. Remember that the scripture says, *"Those who KNOW their God will do great exploits"* Daniel 11:32. Remember that Moses said, *"I don't even want to go into the Promised Land if You don't go with me. But even more than that, I don't want You to just go with me on this journey; I want to know Your ways; to know You."*

Moses had an understanding that as you behold the Lord, you're transformed into His image. God doesn't give powerful and supernatural encounters to people so that they can say, *"Oh, I had this supernatural encounter with God but nothing changed."* Every encounter should be life changing because it's not just an encounter, but it's an

37

experience with the living God. Anytime you have intimacy with God, something will be changed and transformed within you.

As you behold Him, you can understand and believe for the manifestation of who He is in that particular dimension without limitation. For instance, if He shows Himself to you as mighty, you can begin to believe to operate out of His might and strength which supersedes natural might. As He shows Himself as powerful, you can be released in a realm of understanding the power of God, which was promised to the Holy Ghost filled believer. If He grants you the ability to know His vastness, something in you will be released to begin to believe for the impossible to become possible and the unseen to be seen. Nothing can hold you back.

It will be God unleashed in your life; nothing can keep you from what God has said He wants from your life as you live a purpose filled life. The gateway to experiencing deity without limits and to do exploits is to KNOW HIM.

"One generation shall praise thy works to another, and shall declare thy mighty acts." Psalm145:4 (KJV)

The word "declare" means *"to make known, speak of plainly; to promise; to report, or to manifest; to be a messenger of a report of something that's taking place."*

So what will one generation of believers declare to another? God's mighty acts. Would you like for the Lord to use your life as a vessel to declare the mighty acts of God? God is looking for those for whom He can show Himself strong and begin to do mighty acts and exploits.

What is a mighty act? Well, a mighty act is something that is bigger than what we can do in and of ourselves. A miracle that defies logic and confronts the unbeliever's doubt in the sovereignty of God is a mighty act.

The Lord is looking for people who are fully surrendered so that He can declare in their lives what only HE can do. We do not serve a powerless God so why do we live as powerless people.

As a result, we see very few healings or revivals. Although we might not be a vindicated prophet with an infallible ministry, God's Word is still powerful if spoken in faith. Let's be honest, people are tired of hearing about the mighty acts of God in days gone by; they are desperately hungry to see the mighty acts of God going on in His bride today! Don't you want to be a candidate for God's mighty acts? Don't you want to demonstrate the power of God in your life, not only talk about it? With a consecrated life backed by prayer we can see the hand of God still performing mighty works among His people. 2 Chronicles 16:9 says, *"The eyes of the Lord run to and fro... to show Himself strong on behalf of those whose hearts are loyal towards Him..."*

We are supposed to do exploits. We need God to show Himself strong on our behalf because we are helpless if He doesn't show up. Stop for a moment and write down the heroic deeds you have recently accomplished. God's men and women of faith should seek out opportunities beyond the ordinary to bring attention to the supernatural power of God. We should be bold enough to say a simple prayer for someone sick no matter who is looking. As the book of Acts 17:6 says, *"These are they that turned the world upside down."* We can design our life based on how we speak, how we believe and how we react to the supreme authority of the Word. Many books have been written on the ability to be healed or create wealth based on mastering thought. These books lay out the secrets of managing your thoughts and manifesting the world you choose to live in. The core teaching of these modern principles is found in God's Word.

Wallace Wattles wrote a book called *"The Science of Getting Rich."* This book started off by saying a person should start off every day by saying three times, *"I can do ALL THINGS through Christ which strengthens me."* Wallace later stated that you can have whatever you want, but to obtain it is to want it badly enough that it stays in your thoughts. The problem we have is that we are geared and trained to focus on the negative so it becomes nearly impossible to manifest a truly abundant life.

There is no labor from which most people shrink as they do from that of a sustained and consecutive thought. It is the hardest work in the world. Keep your mind focused on what God has already promised you. The Law of Attraction is that you attract what you think, but it takes action to receive it!

Never feel bad for wanting more. **The desire for wealth or overflow comes from a God living within you trying to express His abundant nature through you. He has no financial limitations!** The closer you live to this Unlimited Source, the easier it is to obtain whatever it is that you are seeking. My challenge for you is to make a decision TODAY to change your thoughts, change your words and declare God's Word with boldness and authority without doubt. Brother William Branham would say, *"ONLY BELIEVE, ALL THINGS ARE POSSIBLE."*

You will see a radical transformation in your life over the next ninety days as favor begins to bring things your way through discipline of thought and unwavering faith. Over the next year, you will see a world manifested before you that was waiting all along for you to live in. Decide today to SUBDUE everything that stands in your way from living a blessed life, a highly favored life, a promised life. Don't just tear down the cobwebs, but get rid of the spider. You are a mighty warrior ready to perform exploits. Your bold endeavor to change such a profound way will inspire others. They can begin to change their lives through a proper course of action and live and unlimited life after seeing your leadership.

CHAPTER THREE

WHAT HINDERS YOU?

Hebrews chapter four revisits the children of Israel's wilderness experience, and it gives us a definite answer to why millions who originally escaped bondage under the leadership of Moses ended up dying without entering the Promised Land. It states that some did not enter because of UNBELIEF. Now, remember that unbelief doesn't hinder God; it just hinders you. It is so sad to see a world filled with churches on every corner and homes with Bibles on every night stand or fireplace mantle, yet we see very little being accomplished even though much was PROMISED. Even Jesus said He did not perform many mighty works in Nazareth because of the peoples' UNBELIEF. Unbelief hinders the blessings of God in your life. What good will these promises do you if not received in faith? People often remain in their circumstances because they have no belief in God's Word as it applies to their own lives.

For instance, we know that it is written that by His stripes we WERE healed, which is past tense. Meaning it's a finished work and all that is required of us is unwavering faith no matter what the doctor's report may say. Many people today have experienced supernatural healing in the face of death when medicine wouldn't work. Their faith began to do a work within that brought forth a physical

43

manifestation of complete healing. I am not suggesting that this process is easy, but it is necessary in order to enjoy all the blessings of God.

Many have set out on a journey to do better, lose weight, get out of debt or possibly create wealth. The early stages are almost always joyful because there has been no tragedy, adversity or negativity yet. It's been said that the best way to learn how to duck is to get punched in the face. We are tunnel focused on accomplishing our set goals in order to live a better life. Little by little, bit by bit, a little rejection or a couple of no's and it becomes easy to wilt under the pressure. In just a short while, we are off track and so distracted that we have little to no chance of reaching our goals.

The journey is supposed to be tough. Giants and dream stealers are standing on every corner to knock us down and keep us down. The enemy is constantly whispering in our ears, just give up, those other people got lucky, it's too hard, who do you think you are and it's not meant for you. Isaiah 53 says, *"Whose report will you believe?"*

My question for you today is, "Whose report will YOU believe?" Will you believe that God no longer heals, miracles no longer happen, Christians can't be wealthy, economy is too bad for anyone to succeed in business, revival is over, or Mark chapter 16 is uninspired?

Do you believe the report of the skeptic, so called friends, or broke brother- in -law telling you to quit?

I choose to believe the report of *Greater is He that is in me than he that is in the world*. I choose to believe All things are possible to those that believe. I choose to believe that God is a keeper of the promises He has made and if I speak them with faith they will come to pass. I choose to believe no matter how high the odds are stacked against me or how many times I get knocked down, I'm still an overcomer. My failures do not define me, but through my failures I succeed because I keep failing forward. I get knocked down, but I get back up and keep marching forward. My faith does not rest upon how I feel or my current situation. My faith holds on in spite of how things might look. Many approach faith the same way they approach hope. Scripture says that Faith is the SUBSTANCE of things hoped for. Faith isn't wishing or dreaming. Faith isn't what could or might be. Faith already is! When you begin to declare and decree God's Word as part of your purpose or destiny, faith goes forth on your behalf manifesting and creating in order to bring that thing to pass. It's not about what's coming to you, but rather what is coming out of you! It's a SUBSTANCE.

Hebrews chapter eleven is often called the *"Heroes of Faith."* It describes how every great man or woman met the challenges of their day head on and overcame through faith. It is here that we learn that it is impossible to please God without faith. Abraham forsook all to inherit a promise by faith, and Sarah gave birth to a child even though she was past the age to conceive by faith. Noah prepared an ark by faith. Moses left the riches of Egypt choosing to suffer affliction with the people of God by faith, and many stories of faith are told to prove that no matter how bleak it may seem and no matter how impossible it may appear - with God NOTHING IS IMPOSSIBLE. Only Believe.

How often do we quote **John 3:16, (KJV)***"For God so loved the world, that he gave his only begotten Son, that whosoever believeth in him should not perish, but have everlasting life. "* We have the reciting part down pat, but the application of our words is what God recognizes. If you were on death row and a king or president offered you a pardon, a way out of death row, and the freedom of a second chance, what good would it do if you did not accept the pardon? John 3:16 is the same. The power of this scripture to take away your old man, wash your sins with His crimson blood and not only forgive you but forget the transgression as well, holds no value if you do not BELIEVE. Can't you see how unbelief hinders us from living the life we were ordained to live? Doubt will lead you down the highway of failure. Be warned! Doubt never comes alone. It will bring everything opposite of belief and faith. It seeks to keep you contained in a state of mind that seeks to explain away everything, and leave you stranded in a life of ruins where you spend all of your time making up excuses instead of living an abundant life built on faith and action. These taskmasters called doubt and unbelief will surround you with friends who are going nowhere, doing nothing and feeding your negativity with the fuel necessary to keep you bound and feeling like a victim. Doubt will hinder progress, delay all blessings, encourage hesitancy and despair while eventually becoming the nails in your coffin.

Even in the midst of doubt there can be a flicker of hope rising up saying, *"It's possible, maybe, what if."* Faith, although small, can rise to a level that becomes the source of miracles if fed and nurtured. Maintaining great faith may seem impossible, but when you know your anchor holds in the Word you no longer serve fear or doubt. Your circumstances no longer dictate your choices, but your choices now dictate your circumstances.

As little David did, go gather five smooth stones, and with these five stones kill the giants standing between you and your destiny. Take back what is rightfully yours. Create a revolution that compels others to break free from the chains that keep them bound, and join you in your crusade. You serve a mighty God who isn't dead. A God not limited in resources; One that is omniscient and all powerful. You will see that you are capable of anything when you wake up and realize that you are a vessel in which this God lives and dwells. A God that knows no limits is waiting to be manifested in your words and deeds, and you only need faith to express Him. Allow His sovereign Word to come bursting forth through you and watch the enemy coward down. Satan wants no part of a Spirit filled believer who stands on the Word and speaks the Word with unshakeable faith. **Never let your lack of faith be the thing hindering you in seeing all of God's promises fully manifested in your life.**

*"You can never exhaust God's love and mercy to you. You say, "Well, I hate to bother You so much, Father." He wants to be bothered that way. Don't ever think that you could ever ask too much of God. I believe the Scripture said, "You have not, because you ask not. And you ask not, because you believe not. **He wants us to ask and believe that our joys would be full. He wants you to ask abundantly. Ask for big things; don't limit your faith** to some little mustard seed. Get on out there to some other kind of faith, and move out in big things. Ask... Big things are just as easy to receive as little things. You just have to believe; that's all. You have faith, just know exactly how to use it, and it'll be all right. You can put it right to work, and it'll just be fine."* Rev. William Marrion Branham

CHAPTER FOUR

AVERAGE NEVER INSPIRES SUCCESS

"Our deepest fear is not that we are inadequate. Our deepest fear is that we are powerful beyond measure. It is our light, not our darkness that most frightens us. We ask ourselves, Who am I to be brilliant, gorgeous, talented, and fabulous? Actually, who are you not to be? You are a child of God. Your playing small does not serve the world. There is nothing enlightened about shrinking so that other people will not feel insecure around you. We are all meant to shine, as children do. We were born to make manifest the glory of God that is within us. It is not just in some of us; it is in everyone and as we let our own light shine, we unconsciously give others permission to do the same. As we are liberated from our own fear, our presence automatically liberates others." Marianne Williamson

Never be happy with Average!

If you are not angry with your average performance, you can't make change! As long as there is life, there is potential for greatness; and as long as there is potential, there will be success when you create the daily habits necessary to win! Life will never give you what you need or even want. Life will give you what you accept, and if you accept average and ordinary then this is what life will give you. You will see a life of fulfillment beyond your wildest imagination when you choose to control your destiny. Life favors those that live boldly with no limitations.

The talent you have been blessed with is greater than your obstacles. Do not see yourself as a grasshopper in the sight of whatever giant is standing in your way, but identify the warrior within waiting to be unleashed. You were not placed here to fail or conform. Your Creator didn't form you in His likeness and place you here to simply exist and never make a difference. Your very existence declares that God has a bigger plan for you. Your very arrival signified that you are a winner. Our dreams will always be met with resistance and often come from those that are closest to you, but you are braver than you believe, stronger than you think, and twice as capable as you have ever imagined. Greater is He that is in you than whatever stands in your way. Wake up from your slumber and bury the old you that has accepted complacency. Rekindle that flame that once burned bright with vision and expectations. Stop the "woe is me" pity party and realize that you get to decide what you become. Stop complaining because complaining weakens faith. Instead of viewing things as stress, learn to say I AM BLESSED. What you accomplish is up to you. All things are possible to them that believe so dare to step out and do the things others say can't be done.

Growing up in church there was a song that we would sing. *"Oh Lord, I'm running, trying to make a hundred and 99 and a half just won't do!"* I feel like shouting now as I remember singing this song. Its message is clear. We are not here to run this race and finish just short or be content completing 99 percent. Diamonds are forged through pressure; pure gold comes forth out of the fire. Now is not the time to be satisfied with "almost." No more "I almost made it" or "one day" or "someday." Challenge yourself to truly give it everything you've got. Be willing to go that **EXTRA-MILE**. That's what separates the champions from everyone else. One more appointment, one more call, getting up a little earlier than most, staying up a little later than most, a few more reps or laps. It's that little extra that makes the big difference, and most are just unwilling to push a little harder to obtain the very best. You will always meet resistance in your pursuit to dream bigger, do more, and be more. Robert Allen states *"Don't let the opinions of the average man sway you. Dream, and he thinks you're crazy. Succeed, and he thinks you're lucky. Acquire wealth, and he thinks you're greedy. Pay no attention. He simply doesn't understand."*

Have the very best attitude at what you are committed to and you will experience a rewarding journey. Instead of saying, "I have to," I want you to start saying, "I get to." I want you to decide today that you will start doing more than what is necessary at whatever matters to you. You will activate a law in all of these areas that will bring forth uncommon favor in a way you have never experienced before. You will find yourself being promoted at your work or noticed by people who have the authority to reward and promote you. Your team will work at the pace you set when you are an example of giving more in effort than that which is required. By default, you will see the windows of heaven open up and flood your life with blessings you won't be able to contain. It has been said that we are a body with a soul. I would suggest that we are a soul with a body. A Heavenly being on an earthly journey making an impact as I pass through. **I might say that I am an ordinary man**

living an EXTRAORDINARY life because I do a little extra every single day.

Napoleon Hill said, *"The pot of gold at the 'end of the rainbow' is not a mere fairy tale! The end of that extra mile is the spot where the rainbow ends, and that is where the pot of gold is hidden. Few people ever catch up with the 'end of the rainbow."*

When one gets to where he thought the rainbow ended he finds it is still far in the distance. The trouble with most of us is that we do not know how to follow rainbows. **Those who know the secret know that the end of the rainbow can be reached only by going the extra mile.**

We are programmed these days to fit in or conform, which guarantees a life much like everyone else. It's also why 95% of the world trades time for dollars and most live paycheck to paycheck. They have found comfort in doing what everybody else does without realizing the insanity of this doctrine. Now is the time to have a break-through and discover how rich and rewarding life can be when we pursue life relentlessly. There will always be those more talented and smarter than you, but there will never be an excuse for anyone out working you. Hard work beats talent when talent doesn't work hard. You can start standing up and become a difference maker by adopting a new habit of giving **a little more**. Do so as if no one is looking with a grateful spirit, and when you least expect it you will find yourself earning what you are worth! You will discover that there are no limits to what you can do. You see wealth is not hard to obtain when you give something of value in return for it. When you commit your plans to the Lord you will succeed, and when you put forth unparalleled effort you have no rival. Money isn't a miracle. It's waiting on you.

CHAPTER FIVE

ENDURANCE IS A QUALIFIER

"But he that shall endure unto the end, he will be saved."
Matthew 24:13

Perseverance is hard to find these days. It seems like quitting is the thing to do if it gets a little tough or uncomfortable. In my high school football days we would have something called two a days. These hot summer practices were exhausting, but truth be told, they were used to weed out the weak. They were used to tear you down and find out if you would throw in the towel and quit or dig deep and find the strength to fight when you are at your absolute weakest. I love the quote by William James, *"Most have not run hard enough on their first wind to find out if they have a second."*

There is a story told of Jacob working seven years for the wife of his dreams, only to end up with a wife he did not agree to. Instead of being filled with rage and impatience, he worked another seven years to get the wife of his dreams, Rachel.

If you haven't received what your heart was set on then have the tenacity, endurance and determination to stay long enough to get what you truly want. Don't be so easily discouraged because it seems like your desires haven't been met. You must maintain faith that your unfulfilled prayers are soon being answered.

Maybe you are like Jacob and feel slighted. You have served the Lord and been faithful, but it seems like you will never get what you worked for. I am here to tell you that God is not a man that He should lie, and if He made a promise then He will keep that promise. Our reward is often in our ability to never lose hope. The scripture tell us that Abraham and Sarah received a promise that they would have a child even though they were past the time in life physically for this to happen.

So many times we read the promises made by a God who is the same yesterday, today and forever, but if it doesn't happen right away we lose faith. The scripture says that whatsoever things you ask for in prayer, believing you shall receive. I'm telling you that you either believe this scriptural promise or you don't. The promise made to Abraham and Sarah didn't manifest itself in their lives until twenty-five years later, but the Bible says that Abraham staggered not at the promise through unbelief but was STRONG IN FAITH.

STICK TO IT

When things go wrong as they sometimes will, When the road you're trudging seems all uphill. When the funds are low and the debts are high, And you want to smile but you have to sigh. When care is pressing you down a bit, Rest if you must, but don't you quit.

54

Life is queer with its twists and turns, As everyone of us sometimes learns. And many a fellow turns about, When he might have won had he stuck it out. Don't give up though the pace seems slow, You may succeed with another blow.

Often the goal is nearer than It seems to a faint and faltering man. Often the struggler has given up, When he might have captured the victor's cup. And he learned too late when the night came down, How close he was to the golden crown.

Success is failure turned inside out, The silver tint of the clouds of doubt. And you never can tell how close you are, It may be near when it seems afar. So stick to the fight when you're hardest hit, It's when things seem worst that you mustn't quit.

Author Unknown

Paul wrote in Galatians 5:7, (KJV) *"Ye did run well; WHO did hinder you from obeying the truth?"* This scripture sheds light on how the enemy so often gets us distracted or side tracked from what we had set out to accomplish. When studying the millionaire mindset, or the laws of positive thinking, there is much emphasis on surrounding yourself with the right types of people. Persevering and enduring becomes a much easier journey when we have people around us that are encouragers and believers in our vision. People of like faith that are seemingly heading in the same direction we are. Matthew 18:19 (KJV) says, *"Again I say unto you, that if TWO of you shall agree on earth as touching ANYTHING that they shall ask, it shall be done for them of my Father which is in heaven."*

This powerful text shares with us the value of being connected to people of similar faith in order to declare and see manifested the things that we are agreeing on. Wrong people produce wrong results, and the right people produce the right results. Be more mindful of who your prayer partners are. Have enough discernment to look around and identify those that are not bringing value to your life. Those Delilah's that use the art of seduction to keep our minds off of what we know must be done. The enemy doesn't need you distracted forever but just long enough to railroad your efforts. How many highly talented people fall short of what they were determined to do because of a person or persons that lured them in to their state of complacency. It's been said that if God wants to bless you He will send a man. It has also been said that if Satan wants to curse you he will send a man. Paul did not ask, what did hinder you? He asked WHO did hinder you.

Be careful whose voice you allow to influence you. Be careful whom you get in covenant with. Deuteronomy 22:10 (KJV) says, *"Thou shalt not plow with an ox and a donkey together..."* so make sure you aren't the only one always buying the meals or supplying the gas. Make sure you aren't running your race to please those around you or constantly being told things that alter your mood and make you unproductive. If you are connecting with the right people then you are only one person away from wealth creation or accelerated favor.

Rebekah was watering camels in the evening time and something about her character caught the attention of Eleazar. He was ordered by Abraham to find a wife for his son, Isaac. Rebekah went from watering camels to being married to a very wealthy man.

Joseph was despised by his jealous brothers and thrown into a pit to die. He was thrown into prison for a crime he didn't commit and there he met a butler. Through this one relationship, Joseph ended up in front of the most powerful man in all of Egypt to interpret his dreams. Joseph traveled from prison to being the second most powerful man in all the land. In sports, a team could be ONE Michael Jordan, ONE Wayne Gretzky, ONE Babe Ruth away from being a world champion. We are good at connecting with people who are in the same boat we are in, but you can radically change your bank account, favor and blessings by one divine connection. Scripture talks about giving a glass of water to a prophet and receiving a prophet's reward. A prophet's reward is to have his favor. The Shunnamite woman must have known this protocol as she built a chamber for God's prophet to stay in while passing through. In a desperate moment in life, her child died, she had access to a prophet that could raise the dead.

Lord, help us to identify these divine connections and the arrival of these favored people as they come into our presence. Finding one or two that will agree with you on a certain thing with like faith can be hard but very rewarding. This is why Jesus said, *"If two of you shall agree on earth as touching anything that they shall as, it SHALL BE DONE for them of my Father which is in heaven."*

I have always said I like God's math when two believers connect. One can put a thousand to flight, and two can put ten thousand to flight. When you learn to connect with the right pastor, friends, group, movement, leadership, and mentor, you will begin to see nothing can hinder or prevent you.

As much as so-called friends can be the reason you quit or settle, you may be the person responsible for hindering YOU. Can you see the value of being connected to the right people? Remember, Joseph didn't need everybody to like him. He only needed the right person to like him. You have very few rooting for your success, but you will find the strength to finish when you connect with one or two that believe in you, support you and stand with you. One with God is a majority. You are unbeatable with Christ on your side even if everyone else is against you! When everyone says no, you only need a yes from Him. It doesn't matter who or what stands in your way; you will finish victorious.

You will find that persevering until the end and seeing things through becomes a much more manageable process when you make up in your mind it's worth it and truly commit. Your vision becomes reality when you have a burning desire to possess what it is you are pursuing. Be persuaded by nothing that is opposite of what you are trying to obtain. The least bit of negativity or distraction can set you so far off course that it limits the chances of you seeing your desires fully manifested. So surround yourself with warriors of faith. You have no reason to complain about whatever you ALLOW so stop permitting things or people in your life to impact you in a negative way. Dr. Mike Murdock says, *"I choose my friends and my enemies choose me."*

You will begin to attract the right core group of strong believers to help and encourage you to live life unlimited. **Have you ever had people say to you, *"You have changed."*** This just means that you have decided to stop living life their way. Your growth creates discomfort in their complacency, and it will be these people that start drawing away from you. Revisit your relationships today, and make sure you are not connected to people who would hinder your growth. Stay the course, and find the strength that comes from God and His Word to ignite your passion to finish this great fight of faith. Remember, in the darkest of moments that He has not left you nor forsaken you. It is in that moment that you must keep moving forward. Never quit; never surrender; someone is depending on you. Your family is depending on you and your team is depending on you, so rise up and set a path for others to follow. Be that person that is always doing what others say cannot be done. You will pave a way for others to believe that they too can enlarge and expand their territory just as you have.

CHAPTER SIX

YOU CAN'T GROW YOURSELF IF YOU DON'T KNOW YOURSELF

Why do we struggle with our identity? So often we hide behind the identity created by what we do for a living or some title that has been placed upon us. Maybe your identity has been relinquished to coach, contractor, musician or even pastor. It's possible your identity is trouble maker, liar, lazy, or winner, champion, successful, entrepreneur, hard worker. There are many ways one can be identified. We can allow certain things to govern our actions if we are not careful and conform to whatever label has been placed upon us rather than living life unlimited and on our terms.

Christian means to be Christ like. This identity can be altered by ones perception of how we live. Meaning if there is any group that should be living a completely blessed and favored life it should be the believer. We have every divine promise waiting on us to step up with faith and go get what is rightfully ours. However, identity crises cause us to wait on others, or believe the lie that the blessings of God are not meant for us. Maybe you have bought into the idea that

that surviving or just getting by is God's plan for your life. The challenge always lies in our faith or unbelief, action or procrastination; what if it doesn't work versus what if it does.

Let's start with just one of the greatest warriors of Bible history whose story didn't start out as one of confidence or triumph. Gideon lived in a time where the children of God were impoverished and desolate. The reign of the enemy had dominated their thoughts to that of poverty and slavery, and every move they made was done out of fear that they might get caught or lose everything they had.

We are just as guilty sometimes. I see people in certain areas of town or within our churches living in a defeated state; therefore it controls their every choice. Believers choose daily to live beneath their God given rights by accepting their current condition as God's will for their life. The idea of being financially free to go pursue the things we are passionate about no longer exists. Our thoughts are manifesting a life of fear and imprisonment where they once dreamed of abundance and increase. It is a sad thing to see God's royal seed sit idly by doing nothing when they have the authority to live life in overflow.

Gideon was out threshing wheat one day when he heard a voice say, *"The Lord is with thee, thou Mighty man of Valor," Judges 6:12. (KJV)* I can only imagine how Gideon must have felt. Laboring to create wealth for the Midianites and hiding what wheat he could to survive when he hears the voice of God calling him a Mighty man of Valor. So many times we settle for the path of least resistance, and it becomes so easy to just settle. Gideon questioned this calling, as I am sure most of us would do if called to a role of greatness where much is required. Gideon knew things needed to change, but had no thought of him being the source that God would use to bring forth this change. Gideon knew if the Lord was among them that miracles would be taking place. He knew that the enemy would have no hold on them, because wherever God exists there is liberty, freedom, and victory. He understood what God's presence brought, but he failed to see that God needs a mouthpiece. He needs a vessel to manifest His mighty works through.

It would seem that we all say we still believe in healing, redemption, restoration or revival, but like Gideon, and many others, we are looking for God to just supernaturally do it in spite of our weak faith. We wait on some other person to show up and do it for us. I wish you would see the greatness that exists within you. The very DNA of your Creator lives in you, and He wants to express Himself. Instead of stepping up, we quickly look for ways to step down. Gideon believed in God's ability to deliver. He just struggled with the idea that the deliverance would be by his hands. Gideon said in Judges 6:15, *"My family is poor and I am the least of my father's house."*

Sounds like a valid excuse I suppose. Poor is not permanent; poverty is a temporary state that can be fixed with a few decisions as long as one does not have a poverty mindset. Poor mentality is one of the worst taskmasters anyone could have. It will throw you into a state of self-pity and misery. You will start casting judgment on those living in the blessings of God and rename your condition as something holy and God-Like. Our current situation is the manifestation of all our decisions leading up to now. Wherever we are, we have been in control this entire time. We got to where we are now spiritually, financially and physically by decisions we have been making along the way.

63

Why do we make excuses and cast blame on everything other than ourselves for our current state. Gideon wanted freedom for his people and knew God was mighty to deliver, but he personally wanted nothing to do with this battle that must be fought so he began to make one excuse after another on why he should be disqualified.

The enemy's strategy is to keep you complacent and satisfied with average and ordinary. God created you in His likeness. You were designed to dominate; designed to live an abundant life. There is a champion that lives within, waiting on you to take your rightful place. The fight will be great because freedom comes with a price. If you choose not to step up and change the course you're on then nothing will ever change. Go change the story. Start with believing in yourself and accepting ALL that God has in store for you. The only limitations you have are the ones you place on yourself. Luke 1:37 declares, *"For with God NOTHING SHALL BE IMPOSSIBLE..."* so why do we even allow doubt to enter our minds and alter our actions when we already know what has been promised?

"Impossible is just a big word thrown around by small men who find it easier to live in the world they've been given than to explore the power they have to change it. Impossible is not a fact. It's an opinion. Impossible is not a declaration. It's a dare. Impossible is potential. Impossible is temporary. Impossible is nothing." – Muhammad Ali

Gideon was commissioned with the great responsibility of leading his people to victory. He had received the promise that at his sword and the sword of the Lord he would be triumphant, but he still tried to find ways to disqualify himself. He asked the Lord for signs that would prove that victory for Israel would come by his hands. I can't help but to see many similarities in how we operate daily.

It's almost as if God Himself comes down and tells people exactly what they are called to do and how mighty they truly are, but they still look for a way out. They find excuses for why they cannot go defeat the enemies that are holding them back from their desires.

I pray you receive the boldness like Isaiah. He heard the Lord saying, *"Whom shall I send?"* and Isaiah said, *"Here am I Lord, send me" (Isaiah 6:8.)* The harvest is truly great but the laborers are few. Will you continue to view obstacles and adversity as insurmountable odds, or will you rise to the occasion, pull your sword from its sheath and go conquer anything oppressing your mind; causing you to believe you have to remain in the state you're in.

Gideon's army started out with 32,000 and the Lord dwindled it down to 300 obedient warriors. This had to seem like a pitiful site in the face of war, but proved once again how powerful the few can be when they are totally sold out to His will. Gideon turned an entire nation from poverty and slavery into wealth and freedom because he surrendered his thoughts. He replaced the thoughts of insignificance that hindered his progress with the thoughts that God had for him. **We always see our current state, but God sees our Destiny.**

You were born an eagle; you just don't understand your difference. You couldn't figure out why you never completely fit in with the crowd. Your appetite has always been different than the buzzards and chickens surrounding you. One day, you were faced with a great revelation that you always were an eagle. You were designed to soar higher than all other birds and to see further with perfect vision; not live in a barnyard. You begin to see yourself as God sees you. Your current state has no hold on what you are destined to become.

Little David was the least likely choice in the eyes of man, and even Jesus - in the eyes of most - was an illegitimate birth. He was despised and rejected by the religious organizations of His day. We hear the many stories of triumph that give us hope from sports to Fortune 500 companies. I want you to stop being a spectator, sitting in the stands, watching others walk boldly into their destiny. Start competing in the game of life. Pursue the promises of God and the things you want with a relentless unparalleled determination. Start right now by making the right decisions and putting yourself out there to attract success. As Gideon, I am sure you feel incapable and would like to defer this to someone else, but your very prosperous future is waiting on you to go attack life, confront your fear, and recognize you are a child of the Most High. Nothing shall be impossible to you.

When you design your identity by manifesting your calling with boldness, it will create jealousy among some and favor among others. In Genesis chapter 37, we read the story of the brothers of Joseph identifying him by his gift that separated him from others. They said, **"Behold the dreamer cometh."**

I wonder how others identify us; lazy, always late, fanatic, Holy-Roller, liar, dishonest, credible, coach, pastor, athlete, musician, entrepreneur, successful, ambitious? So many titles are designated for people based on certain perceptions or events. We are constantly told that perception is reality. Although this is true, it is also true that perception can be changed by how we act on a consistent basis. Joseph had favor with his father and was known as a dreamer and an interpreter of dreams. Today, we hold many titles, some good and some not so good. We also hold the power to change how others perceive us. How do you want to be known - world changer, difference maker, visionary, man or woman of God, agent of change, leader?

You now know that there is nothing impossible when you believe in yourself and are one with God. You are not inadequate or incapable, but you are an oracle of God called to do His service. He has called and equipped you. Your past experiences that have been holding you captive no longer control you. The Bible calls those that are His, "JUSTIFIED", which means you never did sin to begin with. God has forgiven you, and you now have a new life with new direction and purpose. This doesn't mean others won't try and bring up your past; it means you no longer serve the past but are free indeed. Be the person that changes the perspective of those cheering for you and has the enemy recognize you. May the devil say when you rise in the morning, *"Oh no, she / he is up."*

The scripture gives an account of a group of men trying to cast out an evil spirit, and the evil spirit said, *"Jesus I KNOW, Paul I KNOW but who are you?"* *(Acts 19:15)(KJV.)* In humility, lead your movement with so much conviction that the enemy fears and trembles in your presence. The evil spirit recognized the ministry of Paul because he demonstrated his authority with power and even knew him by name. Start living the kind of life that inspires others to do the same. My identity isn't in my education or lack thereof, nor is it in an occupation, but it's in Christ and Christ alone. From unlikely heroes to triumphant warriors. From least likely to succeed to successful entrepreneur and multi - millionaire. David had 400 men enter his cave in debt, fearful and afraid, but when they came out of his cave they were identified as King David's Mighty Men of Valor. Do not surrender to the lie that it's too late or who do you think you are. You might feel forsaken and all alone. Maybe even unworthy, but I'm here to tell you that because HE lives you can face tomorrow. Because HE lives within you there is no battle to great and nothing impossible if you will BELIEVE.

"Have not I commanded thee? Be strong and of a good courage; **be not afraid,** *neither be thou dismayed: for the LORD thy God is with thee whithersoever thou goest."* Joshua 1:9 (KJV)

"And the LORD, he it is that doth go before thee; **he will be with thee, he will not fail thee, neither forsake thee: fear not, neither be dismayed."** Deuteronomy 31:8 (KJV)

"Therefore if any man be in Christ, **he is a new creature: old things are passed away; behold, all things are become new."** 2 Corinthians 5:17. **(KJV)**

CHAPTER SEVEN

YOUR FUTURE IS DECIDED BY THE LEARNING CURVE YOU CAN ENDURE

Paul commissioned young Timothy to study to show himself approved, a workman that needeth not to be ashamed (2 Timothy 2:15). Jim Rohn tells us that success is not something that we pursue, but it is attracted to us by the person you become.

You will begin to attract success when you put forth the energy and effort to sharpen your skills and become a better you. Our income always levels out to where we are mentally. You are the sum total and direct manifestation of your current thoughts. When our mind grows and stretches it is reflected in our daily life. It draws those things that are in agreement with whoever you are with a tremendous force like a magnet.

We are told that CEO's make more than 500% more than the average employee. Is it because they have more schooling? Are they just more blessed than others? Factually, most CEO's read on an average of four to five books a month where the average employee reads less than one book a year. Much could be said about the types of books one is reading or the mentoring they are getting. Wisdom is gaining the knowledge necessary to succeed without pain; learning from someone else's journey.

Follow the many blueprints laid by successful men and woman to empower you with the knowledge necessary to rise above all others and gain access to areas that few ever dare to seize. Successful leaders are readers. They are constantly filling their minds with the things that give them an edge in whatever it is they are competing at. I ask the crowd in almost every training seminar I do who has read the Napoleon Hill's book, *"Think and Grow Rich?"* The typical response is two or three regardless of the crowd size. It has been said that if you want to become a millionaire then you must learn from a millionaire.

Today, all excuses have been removed because the internet, among other things, has granted us access to a world where the information is unlimited. The scripture even talks about a time when God winked at ignorance, but today the Gospel has traveled the world therefore making us accountable. The same can be said today as related to succeeding as an entrepreneur. Anyone from any walk of life can start reading or listening to Napoleon Hill, Jim Rohn, John Maxwell, Donald Trump, Zig Ziglar, Jack Canfield and especially the BIBLE and consume the information necessary to succeed in today's market place. The resources today are vast. The only thing lacking is a complete commitment to personal development.

There is an epidemic sweeping through our churches and country that has determined that success is like a lottery or a game of chance. Often I hear Christians say, *"If it's the Lords will."* I grow disgusted with the idea that God wants you to live abundant in every area of your life but your finances. Jeremiah 29:11 tells us that the WILL or plans of our Father for us are plans to prosper us and not harm and to give us hope and a future. John writes that ABOVE ALL things the Lord desires that you prosper (3 John 1:2) and Deuteronomy 8:18 tells us that God has given us the power to get and create wealth.

God's WILL isn't that difficult to understand, and you don't have to fast and pray three days to figure this out. We seemingly live for the Lord, attend services frequently, pay tithes and offering, live righteous but struggle in our finances or in business. It's important that we clarify that being holy doesn't equal success in the business world or even at your local place of employment. Paul said in Romans 12:11, *"Be not slothful in business."* In other words, do not think things just magically happen because you say you are a believer. Be fervent and attentive to earning the skills needed to dominate in whatever field you're in. Never be lazy in learning. Pay attention to the clues left behind by the giants in the industry you are seeking to pursue. Do as they do and get what they've got.

The Bible challenges us to not be conformed to this world, but be transformed by the renewing of our mind. Why do we need a new thought process? It is impossible for you to change anything until you first change how you think. As a man thinks, so is he! You will never escape the reality created by your mind. Allow Napoleon Hill's book, *"Think and Grow Rich,"* to become a handbook to give you insight into the minds of billionaires.

The concept seems so simple. The suggested thinking required to obtain wealth and attract the blessings of God into your life appears elementary. Look deeper and you will see that the discipline needed to stay focused on a certain thought without allowing one negative thought to come becomes impossible for most. Thought is the only thing that can produce tangible riches. The INFINITE living within desires to be manifested, but you must surrender your thoughts to His thoughts and your ways to His ways. Make Him Lord of your life and allow Him to take His place in the throne room of your heart.

Jesus said in St John 15:7, (KJV) *"If ye abide in me and my words abide in you, ye shall ask what ye will, and it SHALL be done unto you."*

This powerful text is showing you the authority we have when our words becomes His words. How does this happen? Paul told young Timothy to study. Study what? God's Word so it flowed in his daily conversation. Paul wanted Timothy to walk in his "I AM" state, where Timothy's words and God's words were one in the same. God's word has no defeat. It moves mountains, solves problems, slays giants, confronts all fears, heals, delivers, redeems, and restores.

When you begin to develop your person through much learning and apply the learning in faith and expectation, you will begin to see your value increase; when this happens you can then add value to others. You will never draw unto yourself more than you think you are worth. You do not need a seminary degree to speak God's word with faith and expectation. You definitely do not need a college degree or even a high school diploma to make millions and create financial freedom. If it is important to you then you will find a way, and if it's not then you will find an excuse.

The world is waiting on you to announce yourself. You don't need to pursue money because whatever money you require to fund your vision is waiting on you. Solomon asked for wisdom, and wealth was added unto his life. You will see the Red Sea part and make way for your arrival when you consume wisdom that others are too lazy to acquire. Even Solomon said someone that was skilled would serve before kings (Proverbs 22:29.) Someone who settles will work as hard as everyone else but make the absolute least. You create unprecedented value in your personal stock when you commit to learning more skills, how to communicate, recruit, close, inspire, invest, sell and build networks of people. It reveals the behavior of your Creator. He has been waiting all along for you to walk in faith and apply His principles in every aspect of your life so you can attract His FAVOR. Anyone can become successful with daily applied effort in the right areas.

Start today by never looking for others' approval. Stop blaming others. Stop spending quality time with people who do not add value to your life and are heading nowhere. Never buy into the idea that suggests others got lucky. Discipline your disappointment, and understand that failure is not a person but rather an event. Your willingness to learn in a moment of failure is what makes you a better leader and positions you for true success.

David would have never been king had it not been for Goliath so embrace those moments that most people run from. You position yourself for promotion in adversity. It's in chaos, crisis, and warfare that your leadership rises above the circumstances and identifies that moment as a glorious opportunity to reveal your worth. The world is full of followers drifting through life accepting whatever happens. These same followers have been beat by life and have forgotten what was promised; much less dream. Stand out; don't sit down. Step up instead of stepping out.

73

Hosea 4:6 says, *"My people are destroyed for a lack of knowledge."* Meaning they have no clue what to do or how to do. They don't know the authority they have because they haven't been taught or refused to hear. They are believers only by church membership or title but lack the power of a resurrected God expressing Himself in their lives. If you have the word of God within you and you have increased in the right wisdom and knowledge, then you will experience the supernatural hand of God working miracles in your life unlike anything thought possible.

We need Holy Ghost filled warriors in the market place serving as Joseph, Daniel, and others served to make provision for those believers that can't. We are no longer held captive by ignorance. It is time to make a decision. When you make a DECISION, you will either find a way or you will make a way. The only think lacking in the battle against lack, poverty, survival, just enough or whatever enemy keeps you sick, poor, oppressed and afflicted is wisdom. This is why Solomon said in Proverbs 4:7, *"In all your getting, get understanding."* LEARN, LEARN, LEARN and then APPLY, APPLY, APPLY.

Challenge yourself today to read more of God's Word than ever before with faith that what you read can be applied and manifested in your life as it has in the life of others. Read books such as, "Think and Grow Rich," "As a Man Thinketh," "21 Irrefutable Laws of Leadership," "Secrets of the Richest Man Who ever Lived," "Rich Dad, Poor Dad," "Something Good's Gonna Happen," "Life, Live it to WIN," "The Unveiling of God" and so many more.

This, of course, is not regular education or general knowledge one might obtain from a local college, but this is SPECIALIZED KNOWLEDGE that targets the right thoughts, patterns, strategies and vocabulary of the successful and wealthy in order to create wealth. Thomas Edison and Henry Ford were very uneducated according to modern thought of education. However, they were both very successful and wealthy because they acquired the wisdom needed for specific things rather than random head knowledge that holds little value in the realm of success that can be learned by anyone.

I'm reluctant to use the word education, because it isn't the same as wisdom. If we, however, approached education from its actual meaning, then we would be further down the road from where we are and view learning differently.

The word "educate" is derived from the Latin word "educo," meaning to educe, to draw out, to DEVELOP FROM WITHIN. WOW, that gets me excited! Success coming out of you - not to you.

We are told the Kingdom of God is WITHIN US. Meaning the KING lives WITHIN US. Our education should arrive from experiences of successful men and women who have pioneered paths and figured out the formula to success. These are the vitamins for the mind needed for mature and profitable thinking. It's the insight into the lives of the most successful and simple truths on how to obtain the same.

Your next season of increase is closer than you might think, and your commitment to a more positive belief system will accelerate this process. Start journaling your life from this day forward as you ask questions, read books seek out knowledge from those who have already arrived at where you are trying to get, and you will see a destiny unfold that was waiting on you all along.

"For if you possess these qualities in increasing measure, they will keep you from being ineffective and unproductive in your knowledge of our Lord Jesus Christ." 2 Peter 1:8 NIV

We will become much more effective when we consume the knowledge necessary to attract the right people into our life that recognize our gifts and abilities to create increase. Place yourself in an atmosphere whether it be a conference or seminar where the types of people you need to be connected to are in a higher percentage. This gives serendipity a greater chance of happening in your life.

Now, you don't just become a Boston Marathon champion by saying today, *"I think I'll run the Boston Marathon."* You would more than likely pass out before you complete this grueling race. You don't just say, "I am going to be a cash rich millionaire and have the income available to support the things I believe in," and roll out of bed tomorrow morning with your bank account filled with unlimited funds. Can God pile millions into your bank account? Yes. Will He? Probably not. He abides and is governed by a set of laws that He put into place.

What a man sows, he reaps and every seed brings forth of its own kind. If you have good seed and you sow sparingly, then you will reap sparingly. I would also suggest that before we start learning how to become successful at whatever we decide to commit to that maybe the first thing we should do is UNLEARN some stuff. Our lives have been shaped by the ideas and doctrines of the last twenty, thirty or maybe even fifty years of thoughts impressed upon us by family, church, or society. ***Get rid of all stinkin' thinkin'!***

You have been doing it your way too long, getting little to no results. Most voices that influence you have no track record of success so why would their opinion hold any authority in our decisions. You will arrive at your destination with good mentorship. There will be some bumps and bruises along the way, and probably a couple of scars and a journal of things to not do. Stay focused, stay positive and keep repeating, *"I can do ALL THINGS through Christ that strengthens me."* Philippians 4:13

CHAPTER EIGHT

THE MYSTERY OF THE SEED, THE JOY OF THE HARVEST

"Now he that ministereth seed to the sower both minister bread for your food, and multiply your seed sown, and increase the fruits of your righteousness;)." 2 Corinthians 2:10 (KJV)

1. Ministering seed to the Sower - God gives you seed to sow. Seeds of money, time, knowledge etc. and these seeds are expected to bring forth INCREASE. Be mindful of God's expectation of you to sow seed into good soil. If you sow nothing you are guaranteed nothing in return. Your future will manifest itself according to what you sow. Paul also states that if you sow sparingly then you reap sparingly. Make sure you embrace your role as a MESSENGER OF HOPE and sow consistently. Jesus told his disciples the parable of the sower, and He told them that they couldn't understand the other parables if they didn't understand this one.

God was ensuring them that the seed was good so be an AMBITIOUS sower. Some falls on hard ground, thorny ground, but then some falls on good ground. If you will be faithful in sharing the message then those ordained to join your journey will accept with joy. Be diligent! Your efforts are not in vain. Your season of life more abundant is closer than you think. No believer should doubt the power of the seed they've been given. God's word doesn't go forth and come back void. God has commissioned you to go produce increase. You are designed to be a river of life that flows continuously so the weak and wounded can draw strength from you. A tower of refuge for the battle scarred soldier of the cross to come rest at. Your ministry is your seed. Your seed is anointed rather it is time, prayer, food, clothes, or finances. Your seed is birthed from God's infallible Word and is the source of life unlimited. No seed of God remains dead and unproductive. When the light of God strikes that seed it comes bursting forth and producing the very nature of God. Reading the Bible can be like reading a history book if you're not careful. Reciting scripture with no faith is no better than reciting Shakespeare. You were made in His image and filled with His spirit. This kind of life can't sit still. This life doesn't live in lack or fear. If the spirit of Babe Ruth lived in you then you would hit home runs. If the spirit of Michelangelo lived in you then you would paint a masterpiece. So when you say the seed of God is within you, the same Spirit that raised Christ from the dead lives within you. There must be something about His nature being reflected in your life because every seed brings forth of its own kind.

2. Minister Bread for your food - God is promising to give you MORE than ENOUGH. Psalms 37:25 says, *"I have been young and now I am old; yet I've never seen the righteous forsaken, nor His seed begging bread."*

God will supply so you can be a blessing to others. It's so important to embrace abundance as God's will for you as stated in the word so the blessing will flow to you and though you to others. How helpless we become when we cannot help ourselves much less others. The Good Samaritan is an inspiring example to all of Christians. The question was asked, *"What must I do to inherit eternal life?"* The answer was to love the Lord your God with all your heart and love your neighbor as yourself.

We are told of a traveler who was ambushed by thieves, and they robbed him of his clothes and left him half dead. As this man lay helpless and in desperate need of assistance, he was passed by a priest and a Levite who looked upon him, but both passed on their way. Maybe there was fear that this man's attackers were still around, or possibly his condition was too demanding of care. Maybe they had no time or possibly money to deal with it. A Samaritan passed by and had compassion on him. He saw a need and instead of waiting on someone else to help this man, he done it himself. Pouring oil on his wounds and providing bandage. He put this man on his beast and took him to an inn.

So many times our definition of help is, *"Well brother, I'm praying for you."* This sounds noble and appreciated, but there are times people need your assistance of money, housing, clothing etc. You can't help them if you are broke! Don't be the person always expecting the next person to help.

The Samaritan checked this man into the Inn, paid for his stay, his food and told the inn keeper that he would pay the man's debt when he returned. Oh saints of God, I plead with you to step out of survival or barely enough and start living in overflow so you can be a blessing to your family and others in need as well.

The wealthy of the world are despised by those in lack, but it is these men and women that give the most to charities, schools, museums, hospitals and much more. It's this law of giving that continues to increase their measure. Start with what you have today.

Jim Rohn said his mentor told him to tip like a millionaire even when he wasn't. He was creating habits that supported his beliefs before it ever happened. Winston Churchill said, *"You make a living by what you get, but you make a life by what you give."*

We know there is power in giving with the right spirit. Jesus told us to give and it shall be given back pressed down, shaken together, and running over (Luke 6:38), and in another place He said it is more blessed to give (Acts 20:35.) The Samaritan understood he couldn't out give God. Your season of prosperity accelerates when you recognize God wants you to be rich. Yes, I said it! The Bible declares in Proverbs 10:22 *that the blessings of God make one RICH and adds no sorrow to it.*

Once you become a good receiver, believe all of God's promises for your life, then get out of your comfort zone and learn how to get and create wealth as spoken in the word. It's in this time that you begin to see the laws of favor at work in your life, and you get to start experiencing how wonderful it is to be a help in your family, local church, or community without always waiting on someone else to step up.

Never allow your vision to be altered for lack of income. These actions allow you to break bread to the hungry. Not only can you give them financial support or aid but impart into their lives the wisdom necessary for them to rise above their struggles and live in increase and overflow as well.

3. Multiply your seed sown – Notice that the increase is established on the seed actually sown. Genesis 26:12-13 says, *"Then Isaac sowed in that land and received in the same year an HUNDREDFOLD: the Lord blessed him."* Then it says Isaac became a very rich man and his wealth continued to grow. God's blessings aren't simple math like 2 + 2 = 4, but its exponential growth; its multiplication.

Isaac was commissioned to sow in a certain land. Money is definitely geographic, and money is always hid in and instruction. Abraham was even told to leave his family in order to receive that promised seed. Money is seed and is intended to be sown and multiply. You are sowing seed even when you give an offering. Make sure you sow seeds into the ministry of those who give. How can that soil produce a return if they struggle with being a good steward over what God has given them or their personal finances are a mess? I've heard believers say, *"I'm sowing but not expecting anything in return."*

This doesn't make any sense. What farmer plants seed and expects no harvest? The power of EXPECTATION is what brings your prayers to pass. It's what makes the dream a reality, and it is required to manifest the things you're declaring. It's time you are mindful of the seed you plant and the ground you place it in. Sow seed with great expectation! The Apostle Paul taught us in I Corinthians 9:10 that the person who plows or threshes should EXPECT to RECEIVE a share of the crop. The minute you sow a seed, whether it is a word you speak or an offering you give, you should fully expect miracles to take place. You should expect an abundant harvest to come forth as a result of what you have sowed.

You can break the cycle of poverty when you understand how to give and where to give. Proverbs 13:18 (KJV) says, *"Poverty and shame shall be to him that refuseth instruction: but he that regardeth reproof shall be honored."* This seed sown in faith will be multiplied. Wow, what a revival! If you've read my book, "More than Enough," you already know God's nature is always MORE, ABUNDANCE AND OVERFLOW.

We can see a new destiny of blessings materialize before our very eyes when we start applying these principles and focus on the fulfillment of the promise. Do not accept less than God has already promised. Do not hide the seed or keep the seed, but sow it and watch the supernatural hand of Jehovah God provide MIRACLES.

"Now to Him who is able to do exceedingly abundantly above all that we ask or think, according to the power that works in us." Ephesians 3:20

4. Increase the fruits of your righteousness. - The word increase comes from the Greek and means to ENLARGE. Of course, we are aware of the Jabez prayer as he asked God to enlarge his territory.

Once God begins to lay increase on your life, it literally opens a floodgate of blessings. There is always warfare involved with advancing any kingdom, and the battle that rages in ones' mind is the battle that most people lose. There is a promise here of enlarging your fruit so you must first have fruit. This can be many things, but it also can be income, as tithe was considered the first fruit. You must take the knowledge that exists in the Bible, couple it with mentorship, and apply these principles in places that can actually produce INCREASE. There is no greater financial advisor than God. Isaiah 48:17 (KJV) says, *"Thus saith the LORD, thy Redeemer, the Holy One of Israel; I am the LORD thy God which* **TEACHETH THEE TO PROFIT**, *which leadeth thee by the way that thou shouldest go."*

We have a great teacher called the spirit of the Lord leading and guiding us through the written word. Why do so many believers struggle with the aspect of income? Jesus talked as much about income as He did heaven. The promises are bold and clear regarding God's desire for you to be blessed in every area of life, including finance. The unmerited grace of God is bestowed without any work you have done, and the blessings of God can create prosperity that can surge toward you on a scale that is overwhelming. Apply proper thought and declared God's Word in your current circumstances and you will see the law of *"like attracts like"* producing the necessary things in your life to walk in overflow and increase. Read the remarkable passages that detail what God is willing to do in your life.

"They will not be disgraced in hard times; even in famine they will have **more than enough**. *"* Psalm 37:19

"I will also save you from all your uncleannesses: and I will call for the corn, **and will increase it, and lay no famine upon you.** *"* Ezekiel 36:29 KJV

"I have also given thee that which thou hast not asked both riches and honour: so that there shall not be any among the kings like unto thee all thy days." 1 Kings 3:13 (KJV)

"I will give you the treasures of darkness, riches stored in secret places, so that you may know that I am the LORD, the God of Israel, who summons you by name." Isaiah 45:3

"Yea, the LORD shall give that which is good; and our land (business, investments, income) **SHALL YIELD HER INCREASE.***"* Psalms 85:12

I could continue to express God's willingness to bless you in an uncommon way but none of this is relevant if you don't accept God's will for your life that you prosper. The Lord knows that this income is simply a tool for the believers to do greater missionary work, build schools, support ministry, feed the hungry, plant churches, buy and conduct business in the market place and generate the types of finances needed to truly support and fund our vision. Stop making excuses for what we don't have or why we don't have it. How many bake sales and chicken purlieu dinners do we have to do to nickel and dime our way to get the funding we need to send the youth to camp or build a church.

We must learn to become entrepreners and generate our on income. Decide what you are worth and invest your God given talents in fields other than just being an employee, settling for a wage. These promises of increase and overflow are activated by your obedience. **The fruits of your righteousness also mean the results of your obedience**. This is how God's reward system works.

A lot of men in the world are not believers, but they experience financial miracles applying Kingdom principles. Christians can accumulate provision without bankruptcy when applying the same principles but with guidance from the Spirit of God. What more could God do in the lives of believers if we would begin to change our mindsets? We can change our financial circumstance as we change our words. Starting today, never again doubt God's desire for you to live a prosperous life. John 15:5 says, *"I am the vine, ye are the branches: He that abideth in me, and I in* *him, **the same bringeth forth MUCH FRUIT: for WITHOUT ME YE CAN DO NOTHING.***"

God desires His words and your words to be the same. He also desires to get fully involved in your dreams when you become fully involved in His work.

Allow the omnipotent God that is living inside of you to have preeminence in your life, and you will bring forth MUCH FRUIT and INCREASE. Life on this side of eternity is so much more pleasant and full of joy when the income is available to take care of your family and pursue the things that you are passionate about. It has been said that having money won't make you happy. Well having no money surely won't make you happy. You are going to work and toil and serve at something the rest of your days. It makes no sense not to create leverage and learn how to work smarter not harder. If God rejoices when we are financially blessed then how much more should we understand the freedom it creates.

*"May our barns be filled with crops of every kind, May the flocks in our fields multiply by the thousands, even tens of thousands, and may our oxen be loaded down with produce. May there be no enemy breaking through our walls, no going into captivity, no cries of alarm in our town squares. **Yes, joyful are those who live like this!** Joyful indeed are those whose God is the LORD."* Psalms 144:13-15

Now, that sounds like revival - multiplied crops and livestock. No government system taking what you have worked so hard for away from you. No more feeling like you are putting your money in a bag with a hole in it. Not just surviving, but living. JOYFUL ARE THOSE WHO LIVE LIKE THIS. We are told that the JOY of the Lord is our strength, and this JOY no man can take away.

Nothing depresses a family more than to want to give but can't. It's a horrible place to be behind on bills, in debt up to your eyeballs, just about to drown or always coming up short. Money is a major part of everything we do. When you have no money it is all you think about. It's like being on empty in your vehicle. All you are thinking about is get gas, get gas, get gas, but when you have a full tank, getting gas is the last thing on your mind. You can read scripture after scripture that God wants to see you walk in increase and overflow so your mind is actually never on getting money because you are in a position where you are mastering your money. It serves as tool for blessing others in your hands it serves you and is a tool for blessing others.

May you embrace total restoration in every area of your life. A true transformation of wealth is pursuing you because of changes you've made and prayers you have prayed in accordance to God's word. It is a combination of the former rain and the latter rain being deposited into your life. A double portion blessing much like Elisha received for being a great protégé to Elijah.

"Be glad then, ye children of Zion, and rejoice in the LORD your God: for he hath given you the former rain moderately, and he will cause to come down for you the rain, the former rain, and the latter rain in the first month. ***And the floors shall be full of wheat, and the fats shall overflow with wine and oil.*** *And **I will restore** to you the years that the locust hath eaten, the cankerworm, and the caterpiller, and the palmerworm, my great army which I sent among you. And ye shall eat in plenty, and be satisfied, and praise the name of the LORD your God, that hath dealt wondrously with you: and my people shall never be ashamed. And ye shall know that I am in the midst of*

Israel, and that I am the LORD your God, and none else: and my people shall never be ashamed." Joel 2:23-27

"So shall your barns be filled with plenty, and your presses shall burst out with new wine." Proverbs 3:10

I pray that you experience MOMENTUM like never before. True momentum is established when you get going and keep going. Start right now setting things in motion through word and deed to prepare for what is coming your way. A part of faith is your work, so maintain consistent daily activity without doubt or distraction. This line of action will produce small victories that will lead to big victories. As your life reaches the tipping point and the ball starts rolling downhill you will then move into OVERFLOW. We have already clearly stated all of the abundant promises that God has in store for you. You may feel as if your train is never coming in, that the harvest is never going to happen, but God has multiplied your seed to multiply your harvest. You are way closer than you think.

CHAPTER NINE

DECISIONS DECIDE DESTINY

*"I call heaven and earth to record this day against you, that I have set before you life and death, blessing and cursing: **therefore choose life** that both thou and thy seed may live."* Deuteronomy 30:19 (KJV)

There is a quote by Jack Welch, *"Control your own destiny or someone else will."*

Much could be said about being the person we are destined to be by being the person we decide to be. Every moment is the result of choice; to be positive or negative, honest or lie. To change or remain as you are. The scripture in Deuteronomy sets a perfect scenario whereby the Lord is giving one a choice to be blessed or cursed, die or live.

Although the choice to LIVE would seem like the obvious choice, many choose to die either spiritually or physically. From the very beginning we see decisions playing a vital role in how we shape our lives, which then shape our world. Adam and Eve were told in the beginning not to partake of the Tree of the Knowledge of Good and Evil for they would die the day they did. Every single moment of every day we are faced with having to choose. We all have zigged when we should've zagged, or turned left when we should've turned right.

In the world of income, we either choose to work for someone else, serving in their field, earning a wage, or we choose to control our financial destiny, own our on business and create profits. Poverty or wealth is both the direct result of choice. So many times we make decisions based on the knowledge bestowed upon us by parents or education. So many of us have learned life from similar resources that we rarely unlock our full potential to be all we can be

The Easter Seal 4-10-1965 Prophet William Branham said in a recorded message he preached:

*"Let me say that again. When this Spirit has found you, the individual, and has come upon you, it is the potential of your eternal inheritance that God thought of you and made for you before the foundation of the world. **THAT IS YOUR POTENTIAL.** Like if you ask me for an oak tree, and I gave you an acorn. Now, the--the--the life for the oak tree is in the acorn. Now, but you have to wait till it grows up.*

*16-3 So do we. When you receive the Holy Spirit of God, it's **GOD'S POTENTIAL WAITING UPON YOU** that's already recognized you, and you're sealed by the Spirit of promise of God into the Body of Christ."*

We are the very offspring of our Heavenly Father. His spirit, His nature, His life is within those of us that has accepted Him. The potential is in all of us to do exploits, perform mighty works, invent, create, and express His deity through us. The Infinite within you is waiting on your revelation of how truly powerful you are so He can come bursting forth; revealing His nature in your words and actions. This will pull all the things you desire toward you like a great magnet. The only thing holding you back is you. Decide today to let the nature of an omnipotent God be expressed through you. I cannot stress enough that when you change your words, you change your destiny.

Your words either justify you or condemn you. The power of life and death are in the tongue so be careful what you say or declare. The positive side of this is that starting right now you can create the world you desire through spoken word, applying faith and great expectation that whatsoever things you speak will come to pass.

As you read Deuteronomy chapter 30, you will see that it promised restoration if the people would hearken unto the voice of God and obey His commandments. This of course follows chapter 28, where we learn the value of making the right decisions. In chapter 28, we are told the blessings of God would overtake us. I really love the sound of God's favor overtaking you if the right decisions are made concerning His Word. We are blessed in the city and in the field, blessed coming in and going out, blessed with increase and prosperity, the ability to lend and not borrow and when people look upon you they shall know that thou are called by the very name of the Lord. Your enemy will be smitten before they ever do you harm. They shall come in one way, but flee from you seven different ways. Those that bless you will be blessed, and those that curse you shall be cursed.

We also read that if wrong decisions and choices are made we will be cursed in all of our ways, until the curses overtake us. We will be in debt and our land will produce no harvest. Heaven comes down upon us until we are destroyed. I cannot imagine anyone saying, *"Yes, that sounds great. Let's refuse to obey the voice of God and be a cursed people."*

How many times do we see prosperity or wealth attached to following an instruction, or a reward for doing something; yet our rebellion keeps us locked out of experiencing the blessing and favor of God?

Our current state isn't anyone's fault. We are to blame. Can't you see God longing to grant you access to a season of harvest and uncommon favor unlike anything you have ever experienced? I have made many wrong decisions in my life and received the consequence of pain both on me and my home. The enemy knows that wrong decisions create havoc and chaos along with shutting up the blessings of God. He surrounds you with wrong friends and wrong voices who influence you. Most failures in life are the direct result of wrong counsel. You can unleash God's favor on your life by consuming the right wisdom to make the right choices. Surround yourself with people that encourage and support your dreams and desires. Do you want people to always say...

"She had potential."
"He could've been the best."
"If he would've lived up to his potential."

I want you to start putting aside every weight that would so easily distract you. Start focusing on the things you can change starting with YOU. Start learning and find a mentor that you can see your future in and inspires you. God saw Abraham in Abram. He recognized Israel within Jacob when Jacob was a deceiver. He knew there was a Peter in Simon and that he would be given the keys to the Kingdom. He could see Sarah in Sara. The great lesson learned in the lives of those whose names God changed is that He could see greatness in them when it appeared there was little potential.

In First Kings chapter 18 we read where Elijah confronted worshippers of a false god and said, *"How long halt ye between two opinions?"* Elijah needed that group to make a decision that very day, and life or death came with their decision. We see the cost of indecision and being luke-warm in this book.

Joshua, who was one of God's great warriors, said to those in his camp, *"Choose you this day whom you will serve,"* and then made his personal choice known by saying, *"As for me and my house, we will serve the Lord."* (Joshua 24:15)

Great men and women are constantly making choices that are rarely popular, but those are the decisions that create favor and necessary change. Patrick Henry declared, *"I know not what course others may take but give me liberty or give me death."* Where have the men and women gone that have a back bone to stand up for truth? It would seem we have become a silenced group, incapable of making decisions. We allow others to force their agenda upon us. By the end of this book, along with careful examination through the Word, we must DECIDE to live the kind of life that God promised us. We must be all that our Creator has called us to be or remain a prisoner of others' ideas and persuasion.

We need to toughen up and not be so up and down or wishy-washy. My mom and dad would have been classified as "Tough Love." I don't mean I lived in fear of punishment or that my home wasn't full of love. The scripture teaches us that real love is corrective. The qualities I possess that allow me to push through barriers and obstacles with perseverance came from the tough love of my Mom and Dad. They simply never let me whine, complain or make excuses. A pity party was tolerated never. I wasn't allowed to say "I Can't." My mom would often say, *"Stop feeling sorry for yourself,"*, or *"Crying about it ain't gonna get it done."*

Maybe you had a momma like mine. I learned to be tough, persistent, and the type that gets it done even if no one helps. I was a young married man and hit a financial crisis early in life. My dad listened, offered some comfort and QUICKLY SAID, "GROW UP."

Today, we sometimes listen to the inner voice when building a successful team or business that says give up or quit, or who do you think you are? Possibly your friends or family can be the voice of negativity, but learn to defeat this enemy standing in your way. Way too often do we stop too soon in our pursuit. When you truly desire something you will unleash a will power that annihilates anything standing in your way. So look in the mirror and start parenting yourself and say, "GROW UP," stop complaining, skip worry, you deserve better, refuse to quit, speak Gods Word with unwavering FAITH and go live the life you were promised by a Holy God. You are the very offspring of God, designed and gifted to dominate. DECIDE to live in ABUNDANCE and walk boldly into your DESTINY CALLING.

"But now thus saith the LORD that created thee, O Jacob, and he that formed thee, O Israel, Fear not: for I have redeemed thee, I have called thee by thy name; thou art mine. When thou passest through the waters, I will be with thee; and through the rivers, they shall not overflow thee: when thou walkest through the fire, thou shalt not be burned; neither shall the flame kindle upon thee..... Fear not: for I am with thee." Isaiah 43:1-2, 5 (KJV)

"I have fought a good fight, I have finished my course, I have kept the faith." 2 Timothy 4:7 (KJV)

"My brethren, count it all joy when you fall into various trials; Knowing this, that the trying of your faith works patience. But let patience have her perfect work, that you may be perfect and entire, lacking in nothing... Blessed is the man that endures trial: for when he is tried, he shall receive the crown of life, which the Lord has promised to them that love him." James 1:2-4, 12

Conclusion

What is there to fear? We are overcomers and resilient. We are diamonds, and we know that diamonds are formed under high pressure. Think of how isolated a diamond is in the earth's core under both stress and heat and confined to darkness; waiting on that moment to reveal its true self. And so it is with believers. Those who suffer great pressure, the most agonizing trials, severe losses and moments of despair so great it feels like there's nothing good ever going to happen. You are being carefully formed in that unbearably lonely terrain by the Holy One Himself as He crafts His children, His diamonds and the finished product of His divine love. The English word "diamond" comes from the Greek word "adamas" meaning "the invincible." When we identify that the Christ that defeated death, hell and the grave now lives in our hearts, we can recognize we are unconquerable because of Him. Even death has no hold on the believer. Diamonds are the hardest substance on earth with no rival and resist scratches, chipping or breaking. A diamond can be used to cut through almost anything like glass or steel. They represent quality and wealth. A diamond that has been cut properly will disperse the colors of the rainbow acting as a prism when held in the sun light. We are diamonds cut from the MASTER DIAMOND - which is Christ. We are His craftsmanship and messengers of light and hope. You are currently in one of the many stages of a diamond, but there's no doubting that you are a diamond. God chose and elected you before the foundation of the world. Start seeing yourself as God sees you! I pray that you will never doubt the greatness that's inside of you again. As a diamond, you will endure any trial and cut through any obstacle standing in your way. Decisions decide Destiny. Decisions decide Wealth. Decisions decide Victory. Make a decision today to go live life unlimited.